A Well-Ordered Church

Church

Laying a Solid Foundation

for a Vibrant Church

William Boekestein and Daniel R. Hyde

EP BOOKS
1st Floor Venture House, 6 Silver Court, Watchmead,
Welwyn Garden City, UK, AL7 1TS

web: http://www.epbooks.org

e-mail: sales@epbooks.org

EP Books are distributed in the USA by:
JPL Distribution
3741 Linden Avenue Southeast
Grand Rapids, MI 49548
E-mail: orders@jpldistribution.com
Tel: 877.683.6935

First published 2015

British Library Cataloguing in Publication Data available

ISBN 978–1–78397–073–5

With loving gratitude to
Art Boekestein:
exemplary Christian,
true churchman,
devoted grandfather.
—WB

To all my former pastoral interns,
who have gone out
seeking to bring the order of Christ's kingdom
into the chaos of the world.
—DRH

Contents

Abbreviations

BC—Belgic Confession

CD—Canons of Dort

HC—Heidelberg Catechism

WCF—Westminster Confession of Faith

WLC—Westminster Larger Catechism

Foreword

One of the more remarkable passages in the New Testament Gospels is the account in Matthew 16 of the apostle Peter's confession that Jesus is the "Christ." In the account, we are told that Jesus pressed his disciples with the question, "Who do people say that the Son of Man is?" This was a question regarding Jesus' identity and mission. But when Peter responds by declaring that Jesus is the "Christ, the Son of the living God," Jesus seems to change the subject. In response to Peter's confession, Jesus promises that he will build his church "on the rock" of Peter's true confession concerning him: "on this rock I will build my church, and the gates of hell shall not prevail against it" (Matthew 16:18).

I deliberately use the language "seems to change the subject" because in a profound sense Jesus doesn't change the subject at all. Because Jesus' identity is that of the Son of God, the one whom the Father sent into the world to save his people from their sins, his identity and mission are bound up with the gathering of his people and the building of the church. When Jesus is truly known and confessed, he is known and confessed as the one who is gathering a people for himself as his prized possession. The mission of Christ is to build the church by gathering, preserving, and protecting those whom he redeems from their sins and restores to fellowship with himself and the Father.

What is remarkable about this passage is that it strikes at the heart of any understanding of the Christian faith, or of what it means to believe in Jesus Christ, that leaves the church out of the picture. It is simply impossible to embrace Christ while rejecting his church. The doctrine of Christ—"Christology"—is inseparable from the doctrine of the church—"ecclesiology." There is no other Christ than the biblical Christ, and the Christ of the Bible has no other mission than the building of his church as "a dwelling place for God by the Spirit" (Ephesians 2:22).

For this reason, it is regrettable that in evangelical circles in North America, especially, there is so little appreciation for the integral place of the church in the life of believers. The church is often viewed as a voluntary organization, which may be joined or left at a whim. Membership in a local church is a viewed in no more lofty terms than membership in any voluntary association. Furthermore, professing Christians are frequently quick to join their voices to those with contemporaries who lambaste the church, or act as though they were able to enjoy a meaningful relationship with Jesus Christ without bothering with it.

Contrary to the unbiblical tendency to disparage the church of Jesus Christ, the authors of *A Well-Ordered Church* present a different portrait of the church. Rather than joining the chorus of critics, they go back to the teaching of Scripture and offer a compelling case for viewing the church of Jesus Christ as the place where Christ is pleased to dwell by his Spirit and Word. Proceeding upon the basis of Scripture, and utilizing the wisdom codified in the church orders of the historic Reformed churches, they echo the church's biblical and ancient conviction that life in Christ is imparted and nurtured within the fellowship of Christ's church. Far from diminishing the importance of the church, they are convinced that, if you would have God as your Father for the sake of the work of his Son, Jesus Christ, then you must have the church as your mother. A rightly-ordered and vibrant church is indispensable to the fulfillment of the Great Commission Christ gave to the church, to make disciples of all the nations until the end of the present age (Matthew 28:20).

Readers of this book may not agree with the authors at every point. But if they read with care, they will undoubtedly be impressed with the book's combination of biblical instruction, historical awareness, and pastoral wisdom. They will certainly come away with a greater appreciation for the way Christ is present and active in the life and ministry of the local congregation of which they are members. By providing additional suggestions for reading, as well as questions for reflection, the authors enhance the usefulness of their book for Christian believers and church office-bearers who desire to see the church thrive and prosper under Christ's blessing.

Dr. Cornelis Venema
President and Professor of Doctrinal Studies
Mid-America Reformed Seminary, Dyer, Indiana

Introduction

The Green Bay Packers football team had been a losing franchise for almost ten straight years. They were at the bottom of the standings, and morale was sagging. Vince Lombardi was hired as the new coach in 1959 and challenged to turn the franchise around. He began leading practices, inspiring, training and motivating. But at one point in a practice, he became so frustrated with how things were going that he blew the whistle. "Everybody stop and gather around," he said. Then he knelt down, picked up the pigskin, and said, "Let's start at the beginning. This is a football. These are the yard markers. I'm the coach. You are the players." He went on, in the most elementary of ways, to explain the basics of football.[1]

Every now and then as Christians it is good and necessary to get back to basics. Martin Luther (1483–1546) once said that even as a trained theologian:

> Each morning, and whenever else I have time, I do as a child who is being taught the catechism and I read and recite word for word the Lord's Prayer, the Ten Commandments, the Creed, the Psalms, etc. I must still read and study the catechism daily, and yet I cannot master it as I wish, but remain a child and pupil of the catechism—and I also do so gladly."[2]

The goal of this book is to bring us back to the basics of *ecclesiology*, or, the biblical doctrine of the church. Here we want to say, "This is a church," in the most basic and fundamental of ways. And to help individual Christians, Bible study groups, leadership training, and existing leadership engage in an ongoing program of education, we have included discussion questions and further reading to each chapter. As we lead you through these basics of the church we recognize that the principles we promote are neither perfect nor exhaustive.[3] Nor will they all fit nicely into alternative views of church government.[4] But we believe they are drawn from Scripture and that they do help us to answer the following significant questions about the church.

Identity

The first question we hope to answer concerns our *identity*. What is the church in general? Who are we as a church in particular? Who we are as individuals and as a church is vitally important in determining how we live. It's so easy as a local church to become branded by unbiblical and unhelpful definitions. Do we define ourselves as the only true church in a dark community, and therefore stay in our enclave? Do we define ourselves primarily as a family that has banded together for the sake of community? Do we define ourselves as a dysfunctional church that is barely managing to maintain an existence? Do we define ourselves by our traditions? Definitions do matter. They help shape our identity as well as our sense of what we do. Definitions can also be encouraging or discouraging. But if we as a church understand who God says we are we will be encouraged and energized.

Authority

The second question a biblical ecclesiology answers concerns *authority*. On a practical level, from whom do we as a church receive our marching orders? How does a church make decisions? If we get this point wrong we will have no sense of direction because we won't know who is leading us. Some churches tend to answer this question rather strictly with a hierarchical arrangement that you must follow ... or else. Others answer this question rather loosely; everyone in the church is free to do "what [seems] right in his own eyes" (Judges 21:25). The answer to the question of functional authority matters in very practical ways. Are members of the congregation required to submit to everything a pastor or elder board says? Conversely, is the pastor merely giving *suggestions* in his sermons and counseling? Is the pastoral counsel of the elders on family visitation to be received merely as information or as a word from God? Do the deacons have anything to say regarding the financial choices of our families?

Ecumenicity

The third question is one we don't think much about: *ecumenicity.* The question here is, how should one church relate to other churches? The Bible teaches that there is one true universal church, called by Christ and uniting around his Word (John 10:16). While this church is "catholic" or universal in scope, as the ancient Apostles' and Nicene Creeds confess, it is concretely represented by myriad local congregations. In considering ecumenicity we wrestle with how these congregations relate to each other. We answer the question, "How do we appropriately express the catholicity of the church?" This question pertains to the issue of pulpit exchanges. It helps us come to terms with the level of cooperation that should exist between congregations with varying degrees of doctrinal affinity. It relates to joint worship services (say for Reformation Day or Thanksgiving Day).

Activity

The fourth question concerns the church's *activity.* What is our mission? What should we as a church be doing? Are we fulfilling our mandate as a church? How do we even know unless our mandate is clearly spelled out? How does the corporate mission of the church relate to the particular mission of individual Christians? In other words, what is your role as a member of a local body of

Christ in the overall ministry of the church? Given that every church has limited resources we need to determine whether or not we are spending our personal and corporate energies in the right places.

These four areas of ecclesiology are critical for us to answer as Bible-believing, Gospel-preaching, mission-minded churches in the twenty-first century. As we wrestle with the Scriptures to find answers to our churches' identity, authority, ecumenicity, and activity, the answers we derive will be like the firm foundation to a building that lasts. This biblical foundation will result in our churches being structured in a well-ordered way, enabling us to do things more "decently and in order" (1 Corinthians 14:40). Paul wrote these words to the disorderly church in Corinth whose worship was full of "confusion" (1 Corinthians 14:33). Instead of confusion, God desires peace; instead of disorderliness, God desires order. On another occasion, writing from prison to the church in Colossae, Paul praised good church order and the blessings that flowed from it: "For though I am absent in body, yet I am with you in spirit, rejoicing to see your good order and the firmness of your faith in Christ" (Colossians 2:5). As we reflect upon this solid foundation and structure in the Scriptures, we will experience a flow of vitality both inside the church as well as outside of it in a dark world.

One final note before we begin: Throughout this book we will be basing our arguments on many Scripture texts (see Scripture Index); for the sake of brevity many will be simply noted. We encourage you to delve into these passages in more detail by looking them up in study Bible notes or Bible commentaries such as Matthew Henry, John Calvin, and/or the New International Old/New Testament Commentary series.

Part One
Identity

Chapter One

The Church's Relation to Christ

After I[1] was converted from unbelief, the church I attended had a "baptism Sunday." It was at that time that someone asked me, "Do you want to be baptized?" I had no idea what that was all about so I asked about it. I was told it was my personal choice to express my personal belief in Jesus. When the day came I was told to stand in a line; then my turn came and a microphone was thrust in my face: "Why do you want to be baptized?" Being the cocky basketball player I was, I think my answer was something like, "I believe in Jesus. Let's do this!"

My Christian identity was my own personal thing. I had no idea how I related to my local church. I had no idea how *my* church related to *the* church or its Lord, Jesus Christ. No doubt this experience and blissful ignorance can be multiplied in our day. The only appropriate place to begin formulating our identity as Christians and churches is with Jesus Christ. This approach lifts up the church beyond how things seem in the here and now. This approach relieves us of the temptation of thinking too highly of ourselves as a church, on the one hand, and of thinking to negatively of ourselves as a church, on the other.

The Church Belongs to Christ

Understanding the church's identity as rooted in Christ will also help us avoid a churchless Christianity, in which individual believers are members merely of the "invisible church" while not connected to a local body, and a Christ-less churchianity, in which the church is merely a collection of individuals existing for social purposes. Instead we begin with Jesus Christ, who is Lord of the church in the New Covenant. That he possesses the church and that it belongs to him is taught throughout the New Testament through the illustration of the church as a building. Jesus is the builder of the church (Matthew 16:18). Jesus is described as the foundation and cornerstone of the church (1 Corinthians 3:11, Ephesians 2:20). Jesus' possession of the church is also taught metaphorically; he is the vine and we are the branches (John 15:1–11). He is the shepherd and we are his sheep in the sheep pen (John 10:1–18). He is the head and we are the members of his body (Romans 12:3–8). He is the husband and we are his bride (Ephesians 5:25–33).

In our time of the virtual online church, "every member ministry" with no connection to ordained leadership, and the prevalence of the "just me and my Bible" attitude, it is necessary to hear again the basic biblical message as summarized by the Protestant Reformation confessions of faith: "the visible Church … is the kingdom of the Lord Jesus Christ, the house and family of God, out of which there is no ordinary possibility of salvation" (WCF, 25.2). It was to this visible church and not to any person or para-church organization that Jesus gave the keys of his kingdom (Matthew 16:13–20). Furthermore, biblical Christians believe, "since this holy congregation is an assembly of those who are saved, and outside of it there is no salvation, that no person of whatsoever state or condition he may be, ought to withdraw from it, content to be by himself; but that all men are in duty bound to join and unite themselves with it" (BC, art. 28).[2] The institutional, visible church is so vital! At the same time, in reading the above quotations, we need to resist the pendulum swinging to the other extreme in which we equate the local church with salvation. Every true church finds its identity in the incarnate Son of God—not itself.

We may be accustomed to thinking of individual Christians as being the possession of Christ; we confess, "That *I*, with body and soul, both in life and in death, am not *my* own, but belong to *my* faithful Savior Jesus Christ" (HC, Q&A 1).[3] But, not only are individual Christians bought with the blood of Christ, so is the church as a whole (Acts 20:28). This is expressed in a classic hymn:

The Church's one foundation is Jesus Christ her Lord;
She is His new creation by water and the Word;
From heaven he came and sought her to be His holy bride;
With his own blood he bought her, and for her life He died.[4]

Christ gave his life for his bride, which is the entire body of the elect (Ephesians 5:25–27). This identity-in-Christ has profound implications for the church.

First, this teaches us that Christianity is not just a "me and Jesus thing." If I am a believer then I am a member of the body of Christ (Romans 12:3–8) and must live out my Christian life in a covenantal, church context (Romans 12:9–21). It doesn't take long to realize that life in the church is not easy; other Christians are not always easy to get along with. In times of frustration I need to remember that I am not the sole possession of Christ. His blood has also graciously covered those who annoy, frustrate, injure, and sometimes hate me. As Paul says, "As the Lord has forgiven you, so you also must forgive" (Colossians 3:13) precisely because he gave his life for *that* other sinner.

Second, regardless of our personal view of the church, "as far as *God* is concerned, nothing in the whole world is more precious than the church of Jesus Christ."[5] If we could share God's perspective we would stop grumbling about the church. We would, instead, have a much higher view of the church than we presently do. Yes, the church militant is fraught with wrinkles. But the church is Jesus' wife (Ephesians 5:25–33; Revelation 19:6–9). Imagine the audacity of openly criticizing and grumbling against the wife of one of your best friends. Unthinkable! Why is it that we are so free to grumble against the bride of Christ? Perhaps we forget the implications of our identity.

Third, the church owes a tremendous debt of gratitude to the Lord (Romans 8:12). Our obligation, not only as individuals, but as members of Christ's body working together, is to do whatever we can to glorify him. This urgent sense of gratitude should keep from neglecting to participate in service opportunities within the local body.

The glorious reality that the church belongs to Jesus Christ closely relates to the next principle that describes the identity of the church.

Christ is the Head of the Church

Because the Lord Jesus Christ bought the church in his capacity as the "one mediator between God and men" (1 Timothy 2:5), it follows that he is the "head of the church" (Ephesians 5:23; Colossians 1:18). The word "head" (*kephalē*) when used in a figurative sense refers to a position of authority.[6] The head on your body is the authority of the rest of the body. Decisions move from the head to the body; never the other way—at least they shouldn't. It would seem to be a given that every church agrees that Christ is the head of the church. But the reality is that some churches practically ascribe the headship of the visible church to a human prelate, whether pope, pastor, or board. This is why Reformed churches confessed so strongly that Jesus was the head of the church, not the Pope. At the beginning of the Reformation era, one of the earliest confessions of faith was "The Ten Theses of

Bern" (1528), which began with this statement: "The holy catholic church, whose sole head is Christ, has been begotten from the Word of God, in which it continues, nor does it listen to the voice of a stranger (art. 1)."[7] At the height of the Reformation movement the Westminster Confession of Faith was produced, which said in its original version: "There is no other head of the Church but the Lord Jesus Christ. Nor can the Pope of Rome, in any sense, be head thereof, but is that Antichrist, that man of sin, and son of perdition, that exalts himself, in the Church, against Christ and all that is called God" (WCF, 25.6).

Christ's headship implies at least two important things. First, because Christ is the head of the church, he administrates "as head over all things to the church" (Ephesians 1:22) and he does so "to the praise of *his* glory" (Ephesians 1:12). In other words, the church does not exist primarily for us but for him: "that in everything he might be preeminent" (Colossians 1:18). How's that for a reality check to pastors, elders, deacons, and all church members? As humans we all want to be happy. But Paul's teaching means that we should not expect the church to exist to make us happy. To borrow the language of the game of chess, we are the Lord's pawns. That is, we exist to further his purpose. The frustration that we sometimes feel toward our church may be due to our unreasonable expectations of the church and, sometimes, our lack of involvement in it. On a personal level this means that you and I cannot consider ourselves members of Christ if we refuse to submit to his administration of all things (Ephesians 1:23).

Second, because Christ is the head of the church he also provides for the body. Our minds were wired with an innate tendency toward self-preservation, which is only circumvented in severe circumstances. Similarly, Christ, as our head, is our Savior, our protector and provider (Ephesians 5:24). One of the ways he provides for and protects his people is through the church. If it's true that the church is not primarily about us, it's also true that:

One of God's great gifts to the Christian is the church. [The church] is for us, because God is for us too. The worship, though ultimately for God, is meant for our edification–for believers' edification, not immediate resonance with nonbelievers (though we want our services to be intelligible to them too). Just as important, think of the *one another* commands. Church should be a place to bear each others burdens, meet physical needs, express comfort, demonstrate care, exercise hospitality, exchange greetings, offer encouragement, administer rebuke, receive forgiveness—basically faith working itself out in love. And isn't love for each other the distinguishing mark of the Christian community?[8]

How does the church's identity in Christ address the sad opinion many today have of the church? Paul refers to the church as "the fullness of him who fills all in all" (Ephesians 1:23). The assertion that Christ is the head of the body is the most honorable thing that we can say about the church in general, and about our local congregations. We are not great because of who we are or how many programs we have, but because of who our head is.

The Unity of the Church

As already suggested, our identity in Christ has profound implications for unity within a church and the unity of the church in general. This "vertical" identity of union with Christ forms and informs our "horizontal" identity in communion with other believers. Our union with Christ means that we already have a spiritual unity in Christ with other Christians; and as churches, with other churches. As we will see later, this relates significantly to the way congregations relate to each other (chapters 4–5 below) because ecumenicity speaks, first and foremost, of our identity in Jesus Christ.

In other words, a church is a church because of its unity in Christ and his Word. In contrast to the Roman Catholic Church, identity is not merely found in an organizational structure.

Likewise, a Christian is not simply someone who belongs to the right church. Later, we will address the Bible's teaching on how churches should unite organizationally. But the church's identity is foundationally a spiritual unity in Christ and in the Scriptures.[9]

The church is a "holy congregation of true Christian believers, all expecting their salvation in Jesus Christ, being washed by His blood, sanctified and sealed by the Holy Spirit" (BC, art. 27).[10] This is the point of Matthew 16. After Peter had just confessed Jesus to be "the Christ, the Son of the living God" (Matthew 16:16), Jesus responded by saying that Simon's name was Peter (*petros*) and that upon "this rock" (*petra*), meaning, his confession of Christ, Jesus would build his church (Matthew 16:18).[11] Apart from a solid foundation in Jesus Christ, there is no church; nor is there any unity among believers. If we are trying to be unified based on common interests, personal friendships, socio-economic status, racial grouping, or even a joint mission we are at risk of losing the right to be called "church." The church is unified *in* Christ because the church derives her identity *from* her union with Christ (Ephesians 2:20).

This identity and unity is unfolded to us in the Holy Scriptures. We come to know who we are and how we should live based on the authority of God's recorded speech in the Old and New Testaments. A church cannot be a church if it does not receive the Scriptures as absolutely authoritative. Paul makes the point in 1 Timothy 3:14–16 that the church, which is the "pillar and buttress of the truth," understands how to conduct itself as such a church only from what Paul wrote to them, in other words, from sacred Scripture. Our study of Scripture should never, therefore, be for solely private purposes. The Scriptures are constantly transforming our sense of who we are as a church and "how [we] ought to behave in the household of God" (1 Timothy 3:15).

Dennis Johnson illustrates this point from the Book of Acts. He asks a simple question: "Who needs the book of Acts?" He answers by painting a scenario that may be somewhat similar to our own:

> Churches drift off to sleep. Small groups turn in on themselves. Bible studies and Sunday school classes tread predictable, timeworn paths. Worship becomes routine. Witnessing becomes the work of specialists ... When familiarity breeds contentment and complacency, when good order calcifies into rigid regularity, then people who love Jesus sense that something is amiss. They know that it was not always this way, and they turn to the Book to see again what is truly normal for Christ's church. In particular when our zeal flags and our focus blurs, we need to listen [as Scripture] recounts the Spirit's acts in the Spirit's words.[12]

As we see imitable images of the church in Scripture that have no reference point in our congregation we repent of our sins and humbly talk about our flaws and what we might do to restore our biblical identity with God's help.

The idea of a universal body of Christ is brought down to earth, so to speak, in local congregations. This means that we need to learn how to live a well-ordered life *together*. As a church we need leaders who will guide us in this endeavor. We need to figure out how to relate to other congregations. We need to figure out just what it is we are to do as a church. But any discussion about the authority, ecumenicity, and activity of the church must begin with understanding its identity in relation to Jesus Christ. True churches, like true believers, are rooted in Christ who reveals himself in his Word, and not rooted in our preferences, felt-needs, or convenience.

Questions
Why should we even be concerned to discuss and study the church and its government? Isn't this just a "secondary" issue?

Why is our understanding of the biblical structure and organization of the church important?

What is Christ-less Churchianity? What is Churchless Christianity? How can both be avoided?

Can you describe a time when you have had unrealistic and self-serving expectations of a local church?

In what way is the church a gift from God?

Without being destructively critical, can you identify ways in which the Scriptures may challenge the ordering of the church of which you are a part?

For Further Reading

Sean Michael Lucas, *What is Church Government?* (Phillipsburg, NJ: P&R Publishing, 2009).

Philip Ryken, *City on a Hill: Reclaiming the Biblical Pattern for the Church in the 21st Century* (Chicago: Moody Publishers, 2003).

J. L. Schaver, *The Polity of the Churches, Volume 1: Concerns All the Churches of Christendom* (Chicago: Church Polity Press, 1947), 65–77.

Guy Prentiss Waters, *How Jesus Runs the Church* (Phillipsburg, NJ: P&R Publishing, 2011).

Part Two
Authority

Chapter Two

Not Human Preference But Divine Revelation

The President of the United States is the Commander in Chief of all its armed forces. Yet he resides safely in Washington D.C. The actual armed forces that defend this country are on the land, and air, and sea. But how do the "boots on the ground" actually know what to do? This is where the chain of command of officers comes into play. The armed forces are a disciplined organization from top to bottom, complete with manuals, protocols, and rules.

Over the church is Jesus Christ, who has absolute supremacy. We saw that in chapter 1. But how does Christ exercise his authority among the people of his church? Within his church he entrusts leadership to "faithful men" (2 Timothy 2:2) who act as under-shepherds of "the chief Shepherd" (1 Peter 5:1–4). That's what we will look at in this section of this book.

The question to begin with is, how do these leaders of the church know *how* to govern the people of the church faithfully under the headship or lordship of Christ? This question is especially important in egalitarian cultures like ours, in which we obliterate all distinctions between people and affirm that "all men are created equal." In this chapter, then, we transition from thinking about Christ as head of the church to reflecting on his rule in the church through the means of men, who act as officers or office-bearers, that is, those whom Christ has entrusted with his authority to represent him and to serve in his name.[1] And this chain of command from Christ to Christians is expressed in the Holy Scriptures. The basic principle of this chapter is that because Christ is Head of the church, the church is to be governed not on the basis of human preference but of divine revelation.

The Scope of Revelation

The governing principles of the church have been—and remain—hotly contested. Commenting on this point the twentieth century Christian Reformed theologian, Louis Berkhof (1873–1957), explained that "Reformed Churches do not claim that their system of Church government is determined *in every detail* by the Word of God, but do assert that its fundamental principles are directly derived from Scripture." He went on to explain that many of the "particulars [of Reformed government] are determined by expediency and human wisdom."[2] The *principles* that govern the church are explicitly revealed to us by God in his Word in commands and apostolic examples; the *particulars* of how those principles are played out among the local congregation or even among a federation of churches are applications of these principles. This is why the Belgic Confession (1561) confesses that "it is useful and beneficial that those who are rulers of the Church institute and establish certain ordinances among themselves for maintaining the body of the Church," while at the same time "they ought studiously to take care that they do not depart from the things which Christ, our only Master, has instituted" (BC, art. 32; cf. BC, art. 7).[3] In other words, not every particular of church life is spelled out in Scripture; therefore, the churches' leaders must flesh out the principles of the Word for the edification of their people.

Kinds of Authority

Properly understood and implemented, this principle can help provide congregations with leadership that walks the biblical line between authoritarianism on the one hand and arbitrariness on the other. To say it differently, the Triune God's authority in the church is both restrictive and freeing. It is restrictive in the sense that we have no warrant for introducing governmental principles into the church that Christ has not established in his Word. This is a warning against a despotic approach to church ministry. It is freeing in the sense that even when we don't personally like the way we "do church," if our ways are based on biblical principles we can have confidence in what we are doing. On the other hand we are free to oppose principles in the church that oppose Scripture. No Christian can be compelled to violate a principle of Scripture (Acts 5:29; Isaiah 8:20).

This principle challenges those who claim that the church should be governed on the basis of consensus or popular opinion. Rule by popular opinion can take two different forms. It can be based on the opinions of the past (traditionalism) or the traditions of the present (democracy). Certainly tradition does have a place in helping us understand how other Christians have understood divine revelation. Tradition can also have a stabilizing effect on the church, preventing the havoc that can result from rapid changes that Scripture does not require. Still, the mantra, "we've always done it this way," should itself always be scrutinized by the Word.

A similarly pressing temptation is for churches to establish principles based on what the majority of the people think is preferable. But pure democratic rule is also contrary to Scripture: "In those days there was no king in Israel. Everyone did what was right in his own eyes" (Judges 21:25). Even collective "wisdom" is still government by human wisdom.

In the Great Commission Jesus Christ makes plain that all

authority in the church is his (Matthew 28:18–20). Christ spoke those words to the eleven disciples, those human leaders of his church. They were good and godly men. But they were also opinionated. They were prone to imbalances and carelessness. Just think of Jesus' disciples who thought they were able to drink the cup of Christ's sufferings (Matthew 20:20–28) or another of his disciples who flew off the handle in Jesus' defense, cutting off a centurion's ear (Matthew 26:51). For these reasons Jesus reminded them, as they assumed their leadership in lieu of his physical presence, that the authority in the church was his. He has decided that the church will be a discipling, baptizing, and teaching organism. He further decides *what* the church teaches, namely, "all that I have commanded you" (Matthew 28:20). It is Christ who governs the church, not men; neither the members, nor the officers, but Christ. He has divinely revealed how the church shall be governed.

If the church is to rely on divine revelation over human preference and wisdom to establish itself, the question needs to be answered, "What does divine revelation mean?" It means that the Scriptures are not simply the place where Christ describes the most conducive forms of life and worship of the church. It is rather the means by which Christ exercises his authority.[4] It is no mistake that God's word is described as a sword (Hebrews 4:12)! Paul makes the same point in Colossians 1:18 (KJV). "… He is the head of the body, the church, who is the beginning, the firstborn from the dead, that in all things He may have the preeminence." The word "preeminence" (*prōteuōn*) means "first place." Christ and his Word must have the first place in all things, especially in the church over which he is head. In every instance where Christ's revelation is in competition with human preference, Christ must get first place. The most telling mark of a true church, therefore, is a commitment to see that "all things are managed according to the pure Word of God, all things contrary thereto rejected, and Jesus Christ acknowledged as the only Head of the church" (BC, art. 29).[5]

When it comes to how the church is governed, there will always be tension between divine revelation and human preference. As a segue to the next chapter's treatment of how the church is led by pastors, elders, and deacons, we want to consider how human preference has impacted the leadership of the church.

Biblical Leadership

The first example has to do with leadership by elders. In many American churches since the end of the nineteenth century, the elder model of leadership has been set aside. Mark Dever argues that alternative models of leadership have prevailed despite the fact that the "consistent" leadership model in the New Testament is that of a plurality of elders.[6] One such example is the "Moses Model" of church government within Calvary Chapels. The parallel is made between the Old Testament theocracy and the church. God was at the top, now it is Jesus; Moses was under God, now the pastor is under Jesus; judges and priests served under Moses, now elders, deacons, boards, and assistant pastors are under pastors; then there was Israel and now there is the church.[7]

The "consistent" testimony for elders governing the church is not always clear to us given the fact that several terms are used interchangeably to refer to the governing body of the church: elder, bishop (or overseer), and steward (Titus 1:5–9). The fact that three titles are given to this office is simply God's way of teaching us about the varied facets of the office of church leadership. Similarly, a mother may be called "a homemaker," "a caretaker," and "life-coach" while still being a mother. Each of the titles shows us something of her overall calling. In the same way church leaders are given three titles here (and others elsewhere) to show us the variety of their calling.

Elder

The concept of elder is not new to the New Testament but is borrowed from the Old Testament.[8] Especially around the time of Moses and the exodus we see elders being used to help govern the people and to assist in the worship of God (Exodus 3:16–18). Later, during the wandering, upon Jethro's advice, Moses selected seventy elders to help govern the people (Exodus 18, 24:1). Elders are mentioned during the time of the judges (Judges 21:16, Ruth 4:2) as well as during the monarchy (1 Kings 8:1). Later, during the exile, elders were the threads that held the society together through their involvement in the synagogues (Ezra 6:7). Finally, we read about the elders of Israel in the New Testament. With much carry-over from the Old Testament, these elders made up the Jewish Sanhedrin that governed religiously, socially, and at times, even politically. Throughout the book of Acts, "elders" refers to the elders of Israel until chapter 11 where Luke records that Christians sent their gifts to the elders by the hands of Barnabas and Saul (Acts 11:30). Luke doesn't even bother to explain the term. He takes for granted that just as there were elders in the Old Testament church so there are elders in the New Testament church.

The term "elder" originally referred to the age of the leader. In time it began to denote not age but status. Just as older men are worthy of respect because of their age, so are officers of the church worthy of respect because of their wisdom and experience as well as their appointment by God as the organizational and decision making body of the church (1 Timothy 5:17).

Overseer

Elders are also designated as overseers (translated in the King James Version as "bishops"). The duty of an overseer is well illustrated in Acts 20, which interchangeably speaks of the elders as overseers (Acts 20:17, 28), whose task it was to watch over the church (Acts 20:28–31). In Acts 20:28, overseers are also called to feed or shepherd the flock. A shepherd assumes responsibility for the well being of the flock. Toward that end he scans the horizon for impending threats, he identifies and addresses injuries among the sheep, he leads them to green pastures. Christ is the Shepherd and Overseer of our souls. He is the great Bishop (1 Peter 2:25). But in God's infinite wisdom he has delegated the oversight of the church on earth to his officers. The bishop acts on behalf of Christ. Elders and pastors have been called by God to oversee the flock. In our day this is not often appreciated. We don't like people looking over us. No doubt, this is why many churches today do not have elders. But God has given overseers, bishops, for our good. They are to look out for doctrinal, practical, and societal dangers and use God-given means to protect us from these.

Something must be said about the relationship (or lack thereof) between the biblical conception of a bishop and the Roman Church's conception of a bishop. In the Roman Church, "bishop" is a title given to a man who has charge over a number of priests and who is himself subject to the Pope. But, nowhere in the Bible is warrant given for a hierarchical conception of church leadership. In Acts 20:28 we notice that there are several bishops in the same congregation with no noted distinction. In the Bible bishops were godly men, called by God through the local church to rule the local church; nothing more, nothing less.

Steward

Elders are also described as "stewards" (Titus 1:7; *oikonomon*). Literally this means they are managers of a house. The biblical concept of a steward is described in Luke 12:37–48. The manager protects his house and guards against break-ins. He is called to be watchful, faithful, and wise. But in 12:43 this steward is called a servant: "The steward in the New Testament is a steward from among slaves, who is over the whole household and sometimes over the whole property of his master."[9] The steward, the administrator of the house, himself has a Lord (12:43). The manager of a business is beneath the owner of the business. God is the Lord of his church. But he has appointed stewards—managers—to govern his church in his earthly absence.

What do we learn about church leaders by virtue of their role as household managers or rulers? They are merely the keepers of *God's* mysteries (1 Corinthians 4:1). In Corinth, some people were boasting in their minister. Paul reminds them that they are merely stewards in a position of servitude not of self-promoting glory. As one writer said, "The office-bearers represent not the Church, but Christ, just as in a monarchy the functionaries represent the monarch."[10] The church is not a democracy. It is a representative monarchy. God is the monarch and he, through the church, chooses leaders to represent him. John Calvin (1509–1554) pointed out that "God has determined ... to govern his Church by the ministry of men, and indeed frequently selects the ministers of the Word from among the lowest dregs of the people." Nonetheless, "the testimony of our salvation, when delivered to us by men whom God has sent, is not less worthy of credit, than if His voice had resounded from heaven."[11] Rule by fallen men teaches us God's condescension. He meets with his people and communicates to them through those who are like us. It also teaches us humility and promotes true faith and piety. Some might say, "I would believe in and submit to Christ if he came and spoke to me himself." But God chooses to build us up in a way that challenges our faith.

This brief examination of elders as God's plan for church leadership should challenge the claim made by somewhat Calvinistic evangelicals that a presbyterian (rule by elder) model is merely patterned after secular organization.[12]

Gender

Another example of how human preference can compete with God's plan for leadership in the church is the ongoing question of whether or not God has called only men to be in the official positions of leadership in the church. Increasingly, despite the church's nearly uncontested understanding that Acts 6:3, 1 Timothy 3:2, 12, and Titus 1:6 restrict these offices to men, the assumption is that women should be church leaders too. It is no coincidence that calls for women to be admitted to all levels of Christian office in historic Reformed denominations in America followed on the heels of the tumultuous social upheavals of the 1960s.

All of this is not to say that there is no place for human preference in the church (color of carpet, size of pulpit etc.). Tim Keller has rightly argued that we need to be careful to avoid confusing divine revelation with human preferences.[13] Sometimes what we claim to be divine revelation is simply personal preference, or convictions regarding the perceived consequences of scriptural statements. But where God has given instructions, his Word is our marching orders. The Church is the possession of Christ. Christ is the head of the church. Because of this relationship we cannot determine who we are or how we operate as a Church. This prerogative belongs to God who must reveal it to us. Thankfully, Christ has spoken and what he revealed in speech was recorded in words, telling us just how he will care for his church.

Questions

Why will there always be conflict between divine revelation and human preference?

Why is it important to clearly distinguish between divine revelation and human preference?

In what ways do the Scriptures govern the church's government?

How does the Great Commission relate to church government?

Why does the New Testament not offer extended argument demonstrating that the church should be governed by elders, or more specifically, male elders?

How might the role of a church leader as an overseer cause western Christians to recoil?

For Further Reading

Daniel R. Hyde, "Rulers and Servants: The Nature of and Qualifications for the Offices of Elder and Deacon," in *Called to Serve: Essays for Elders and Deacons*, ed. Michael G. Brown (Grandville: Reformed Fellowship, 2007), 1–16.

D. Martyn Lloyd-Jones, *Authority* (Edinburgh: The Banner of Truth, 1997).

Herman Ridderbos, *Studies in Scripture and its Authority* (Grand Rapids: Eerdmans Publishing Co., 1978).

Chapter Three

Christ Ministers Through Officers

The Lord's Day service and fellowship afterwards was particularly sweet. There was a "buzz" of gospel excitement as well as enthusiasm with several new worshipers. In one new family, everyone seemed to have enjoyed the service—except the husband. He looked like a superhero; he was obviously a Marine. In talking with the family the wife asked about membership, as they had just moved from a previous deployment and previous church and wanted to settle in. I asked where they were coming from and the wife proceeded to mention the city and the church where she was a member. Curious to hear from the husband I asked him, "Are you a member of the same church?" He answered: "I don't believe in church membership. I'm a member of the invisible church." A lengthy conversation ensued that went nowhere. I ended the conversation with a challenge to him: "You're a Christian, but do not belong to a local church of Jesus Christ; you're a Marine, so does that mean you belong to the invisible Marines?"

The concept of authority is extremely important, especially in the time and place in which we live. Owing partly to Western democratic ideals and partly to the real and perceived independence that our affluence affords us we live in an age that resists external intrusion into our lives. We have an unspoken "Don't Ask Don't Tell" policy in the visible church: "No one has any business asking me about my walk with God and they certainly have no business telling me what to do about it." No doubt you've heard something like this. You may have even said it!

Of course, there is nothing strictly modern about anti-authoritarian sentiments. This is the ancient error: "Hath God said?" (Genesis 3:1; KJV). Later, almost immediately after the Lord chose Moses to lead his people out of Egypt one of the Israelites challenged him saying, "Who made you a ruler and a judge over us? (Acts 7:27). Strikingly, just a few verses later in Luke's account of this Old Testament story we read, "This Moses, whom they rejected, saying, 'Who made you a ruler and a judge?'—this man *God sent as both ruler* and redeemer by the hand of the angel who appeared to him in the bush" (Acts 7:35). One of the most significant of all Israel's divinely appointed leaders was originally and repeatedly rejected by his own people. Is it any wonder, then, that when the Lord himself came from heaven to earth, John said, "He came unto his own, and his own received him not?" (John 1:11; KJV)

This same power struggle exists today in your heart and in mine, even after we have come under the lordship of Jesus Christ. We all have a sinful desire to be autonomous. But in response to that age-old objection, "Who made you a ruler over us," Jesus Christ has given an answer in his Word: He governs and guides his church through office-bearers whom he chooses.

Later we'll see just *how* it is that *Christ* cares for his church through officers. For now, we want to focus on the idea that those the church chooses as its office-bearers were appointed by Jesus Christ himself to represent him. This is extremely important. The pastors, elders, and deacons are neither employees of the church nor elected officials to do the bidding of the church. They are God's officers chosen by him to care for the church.

Does God Really Choose Office-Bearers?

One way to demonstrate that church officers are God's chosen instruments is to see what Paul says about earthly leaders in general in Romans 13:1–7. The fact that these verses are written explicitly concerning *civil* authorities cannot be used as an objection to their application in the church, because of the comprehensive scope of the words used. In verse 1 Paul says, "Let *every* (*pasa*) person be subject to the governing authorities. For there is *no* authority *except* from God, and those that exist have been instituted by God" (Romans 13:1; emphasis added). Understanding God's sovereignty the way the Bible presents it, we can say that every governing authority from president to pastor to parent has been chosen by God for that position. As Paul says, the governing authorities are actually "God's servants" or ministers (Romans 13:4; *diakonos*).

More specifically, God chooses officers *for* his church through his Word and Spirit working *in* the church. The Belgic Confession outlines the biblical procedure for calling a man to an office, saying, it must be "by a lawful election by the Church, with calling upon the name of the Lord, and in that order which the Word of God teaches" (BC, art. 31).[1]

God provides specific criteria in his Word, apart from which, no one should be called to an office (Exodus 18:21; 1 Timothy 3). The officers of the church, through the Spirit's guidance and scriptural mandate separate other men to fill positions in the church. While the officers of a congregation must make final decisions concerning the spiritual care of their people (Titus 1:5) they must also take into consideration the sentiments of the congregation (Acts 6:2–3). These officers are elected by the congregation, as both the Old (Exodus 18; Leviticus 8:4–6; Numbers 20:26–27; Deuteronomy 1:13–15) and New Testaments indicate (Acts 1:12ff.; 6:3, 5, 6;

2 Corinthians 8:19). As Acts 14:23 relates, the elders in Lystra, Derbe, Iconium, and Antioch were "elected by a show of hands" (Greek, *cheirotoneō*).[2] These officers are then ordained and installed by the laying on of hands and prayer (Acts 6:6; 13:1–3; 1 Timothy 4:14; 2 Timothy 1:6). The end result is that God chooses officers by means of his church: "*He himself* gave some to be ... pastors and teachers..." (Ephesians 4:11, 12; cf. 2 Corinthians 5:20). The form for ministerial ordination in the churches in which we serve exhorts the congregation to, "Submit to those whom *God has placed* over you, for they care for you as those who shall give account."[3] Our form for the Ordination of Elders and Deacons also asks those to be ordained, "Do you, both elders and deacons, feel in your hearts that you are lawfully called of God's church, *and consequently of God Himself*, to these your respective offices?" (emphasis added).[4]

Who are the Officers that God Chooses?

The New Testament speaks of the church being governed by officers, namely, by ministers or pastors, elders, and deacons (1 Timothy 3; cf. BC, art. 30). The elders and pastors together are God's means of managing, overseeing, shepherding, and counseling the church of God: "The [shepherds] set the agenda and clarify the vision for every aspect of a church's ministry."[5] Understanding the relationship between pastors and elders is extremely important. Contrary to the practice in some churches, pastors are not below the elders. In fact, the pastor, or teaching elder, is mentioned in 1 Timothy 5:17 as worthy of distinct honor among the elders. A pastor is an elder but his calling is distinct enough to warrant a distinct office for the sake of clarity.[6] Neither should the pastor dominate over the other elders, who are among the flock he shepherds as Peter says:

> So I exhort the elders among you, as a fellow elder and a witness
> of the sufferings of Christ, as well as a partaker in the glory that
> is going to be revealed: shepherd the flock of God that is among
> you, exercising oversight, not under compulsion, but willingly,

as God would have you; not for shameful gain, but eagerly; not domineering over those in your charge, but being examples to the flock. (1 Peter 5:1–3)

When Peter addresses the elders (*presbuterous*) he goes on to call himself a "fellow elder" (*sumpresbuteros*), a word unique in Greek literature to Peter. By calling himself this he was identifying with these elders in their work of shepherding and not lording his apostleship over them.[7]

In Acts 6, we learn that those set apart as servants in the church were appointed to assist its teaching ministry; their unique servant-calling would later become the office known as the diaconate. The apostles laid their hands upon the deacons indicating their recognition as Christ's officers. They are named in Philippians 1:1 along with the overseers as being officers in Christ's church. The deacons are responsible for the care of widows and the poor, and particularly those widows and poor of the church (Acts 6:1–2; Galatians 6:10). Deacons are not hired custodians or accountants. The deacons represent Christ: "The office of the deacons is the office in which Christ continues his priestly work."[8] That is, Christ performs his works of unmerited mercy through the deacons just as the priests did with the diseased and poor in Israel.[9] Again, to quote from the ordination form in the churches in which we serve, "The office of deacon is based upon the interest and love of Christ in behalf of his own."[10] Thus, as Christ's official ministers of mercy, the deacons must live out their obligation to be "full of the Spirit and of wisdom" (Acts 6:3).

In this capacity, the diaconate helps to substantiate the preaching of the free grace of the gospel of Christ, not because they have the authority to preach or to rule but the authority to administer charity on behalf of the loving Christ.[11] Just as the disciples were to go out preaching and healing, so the church today preaches through the pastors and offers physical relief through the deacons.[12]

When they work in harmony, deacons free pastors to preach, leading to the blessing of God upon the Word, multiplying believers (Acts 6:7). As an aside, this is why, in most cases, the deacons of a church offer gifts to those in need, not loans. A loan does not help proclaim the free grace of the gospel. It rather proclaims the opposite position of servitude (Proverbs 22:7). When the deacons offer a gift they can say, "This is a cup of cold water offered in the name of Christ. Go and use it to God's honor and glory." I have seen grown men weep out of joy and gratitude when the deacons freely offer them assistance in Jesus' name. For this reason, "A well-ordered diaconal ministry is vital for the church's proclamation of the gospel of God's grace."[13]

Practical Implications of the Leadership of Elders and Deacons

What does all this mean in practice? First, God's officers are not just figureheads. They need to be real shepherds. Critics of elder ecclesiology point out that elders are usually good businessmen who are generally godly but may not always be skilled shepherds of souls who merely function more like a corporate board.[14] We need to listen to this critique; no doubt there is much anecdotal evidence to support it. But it does not have biblical evidence. Acts 20 does not present local leaderships merely in terms of ruling but also in terms of guiding and teaching. Elders are not merely decision-makers. Pastors are not merely disseminators of biblical information. Deacons are not merely providers of physical assistance. All of God's officers are charged to exercise genuine and costly care for the church. They are to care for the bodies and souls of the individuals in the church. They must take heed to the well-being and witness of the congregation as a whole. And they must have a regard for the universal church of God. The Church Order of the federation of churches in which we minister emphasizes this spiritual task of church office by listing "continuing in prayer" as the first duty of the minister, elder, and deacon.[15] It is very easy for elders and pastors to complain about the state of the church they are called to lead. But godly leaders recognize themselves as the change-agents and vision setters of the church. If the leaders will not take responsibility for the faults in a congregation who will? A helpful diagnostic question to determine the quality of shepherding in a congregation is this: "Do the pastors, elders, and deacons regularly visit their members to check up on their spiritual and physical well-being?"

Second, the officers of God's Church should be honored (1 Timothy 5:17). This is true of the deacons as well as the pastors and elders. It is our firm conviction that the ministry of the deacons is not honored as it should be today. Probably because money is seen as a personal matter many deacons have to walk on eggshells when they give financial counsel. Isn't it ironic that people will call in to a radio show to ask for financial advice but will rarely ask the same advice from one of the deacons that knows them? Furthermore, the financial advice of a radio show personality is probably more likely to be *heeded* that that of a deacon.

Imagine if the deacons of your church approached you and said with love and compassion, "We are concerned about your financial priorities. Your car-payments are competing with your tithing. You have gotten yourself into consumer debt contrary to the counsel of God. We believe you should take a few semesters off of college to learn financial responsibility." How would you respond? Can you hear yourself saying, "Who made you a ruler and judge over me?" As we've learned, it is God himself who cares for his church through his officers.

Or imagine this scenario. You apply for help from the deacons, which is something that every member of a Christian church should feel comfortable doing. When you do, they hand you an application form. This form asks you to fill out a budget itemizing your expenses, including giving as well as your income. In response you ask, "Who are *you* to ask these questions?" They answer: "We are God's ministers."

As deacons are to be honored, so too, are pastors and elders. The low view of the pastorate today is evidenced by the way that members speak to and about their pastors, the way their guidance is too-often dismissed or not sought at all, and in too many cases, the way they are compensated for their labors. Yet God says to honor them (1 Timothy 5:17–18; Hebrews 13:7). As one sixteenth-century confession asserts: "Moreover, in order that this holy ordinance of God may not be violated or slighted, we say that every one ought to esteem the ministers of God's Word and the elders of the Church very highly for their work's sake, and be at peace with them without murmuring, strife, or contention, as much as is possible" (BC, art. 31).[16] Similarly, the form for ordination of ministers in our churches contains this scripture-laden phrase:

> And you likewise, beloved Christians, receive this your minister in the Lord with all joy; and hold such in honor. Remember that God Himself through him speaks unto you and entreats you. Receive the Word, which he, according to the Scripture, shall preach unto you, not as the word of men, but, as it is in truth, the word of God. Let the feet of them that preach the gospel of peace, and bring good tidings of good, be beautiful and pleasant to you. Obey them that have the rule over you, and submit to them; for they watch in behalf of your souls, as they that shall give account; that they may do this with joy, and not with grief: for this were unprofitable for you.

The paragraph concludes on this note of encouragement:

> If you do these things, it shall come to pass that the peace of God shall enter your houses, and that you who receive this man in the name of a prophet, shall receive a prophet's reward, and

through his preaching believing in Christ, shall through Christ inherit eternal life.[17]

The form for ordination of elders and deacons concludes similarly:

> I charge you, beloved Christians, to receive these brethren as the servants of God, sustaining them with your daily prayers. Render to the elders all honor, encouragement, and obedience in the Lord. Provide the deacons generously with the necessary gifts for the needy, remembering that in so much as you do it unto the least of these His children, you do it unto Him. May God give us to see in the ministry of the elders the supremacy of Christ, and in the ministry of the deacons, the care and love of the Savior.[18]

How we heed the authority in the church is a reflection of how we heed God's authority. The fact is, the church that resists authority is neither well-ordered nor healthy. There is no doubt that the low level of respect for God's officers in some circles today stems from a low level of morality demonstrated by some of the churches' officers. We should remember, though, that our faithfulness does not depend upon the faithfulness of other fallen men. The good news, even when the view and state of the offices declines is that *Christ cares for his church* through the officers he chooses. The result of receiving this leadership is not only a well-ordered church but also great joy and eternal life.

Questions

Why is it so difficult for us to submit to authorities? How might this difficulty impact the health of your church?

Interact with the statement: "God chooses the officers for this church."

Briefly describe the offices of elder and pastor. What is the relationship between the two?

Briefly describe the office of deacon. What is their relationship to the ministry of the Word?

Of what significance should it be to an officer that God has chosen him to care for the church?

Of what significance should it be to a non-officer that God chooses officers to care for his church?

For Further Reading

Peter Y. De Jong, *Taking Heed to the Flock: A Study of the Principles and Practice of Family Visitation* (1948; reprinted, Eugene, OR: Wipf & Stock, 2003).

——, *The Ministry of Mercy for Today* (1952; reprinted, Eugene, OR: Wipf & Stock, 2003).

William Heyns, *Handbook for Elders and Deacons: The Nature and the Duties of the Offices According to the Principles of Reformed Church Polity* (Grand Rapids: Wm. B. Eerdmans Publishing Company, 1928), 13–30.

J. L. Schaver, *The Polity of the Churches, Volume 1: Concerns All the Churches of Christendom* (Chicago: Church Polity Press, 1947), 133–176.

Part Three
Ecumenicity

Chapter Four

Within a Denomination

I was a stranger in a different hemisphere, on a different continent, in a different country, among people who spoke a different language. Have you ever had that feeling? Then the music began to play a familiar tune. Then they began to sing in their unknown tongue yet I found myself singing along from the projected words on the screen:

> Não fosse Deus, que_o diga Israel,
> Se_ao nosso lado não viesse_estar,
> Quando se_ergueram homens contra nós,
> Com toda ira vindo sobre nós,
> Vivos seriamos tragados, pois.

There we were in the summer of 2011 in Maragogi, Brazil, singing to the sixteenth century Genevan tune known to us as "Old 124th," the words of the three thousand year old Psalm 124, which I knew as:

> Now Israel may say, and that in truth,
> If that the Lord had not our right maintained,
> If that the Lord had with us remained,

When cruel men against us rose to strive,
We surely had been swallowed up alive.[1]

That's catholicity. And catholicity leads us the topic of
ecumenicity, that is, how local churches are to relate to other
churches all as members of the universal or catholic church?

The term *ecumenical*, simply refers to the unity that exists among
the churches that make up the body of Christ. It comes from
a Greek word meaning "worldwide" (*oikoumenē*). The position
taken and defended in this chapter is that while diverse local
congregations are each manifestations of the one Body of
Christ, they are also members of the whole and therefore rather
than remain independent or isolated, should unite together in
some form of covenantal relationship with other like-minded
congregations. In the words of Herman Bavinck (1854–1921),
"Every local church is therefore simultaneously an independent
manifestation of the body of Christ *and* part of a larger whole."[2]

It should become clear in the paragraphs to follow, however,
that it is not enough to merely join a federation. It is also essential
to have a proper understanding of how to function within a
federation of churches. In other words, this section has to do with
the principles and practice of church association and cooperation.
While this topic may only seem to hold relevance for the church
"higher-ups," the truth is, it is a very practical issue. How your local
congregation relates to other congregations within the broader
church sets a pattern for how believers from one church will relate
to those from another. The rigid exclusivity of some churches can
breed pride and narrowness in its members. On the other hand, the
ecclesiastical promiscuity of other churches can leave its members
unable or unwilling to draw up theological boundaries in their
personal lives.

A Key Distinction

In this section, we will make a distinction between federative relationships (chapter four) and ecumenical cooperation (chapter five). The principle underlying this distinction is that the level of cooperation and unity shared between Christian churches will be in proportion to their theological (and even geographical and cultural) kinship. Congregations will be in organic union with congregations closest to them. But whether in a denomination or not, every church should think carefully about how it relates to those outside its organic community.

A Key Definition

Throughout this chapter the terms "denomination" and "federation" will be used interchangeably; "network" is probably the closest contemporary synonym. We realize that not everyone will agree with our assessment and that all of these titles have inherent liabilities.

We affirm that "denomination" carries the negative connotation of hierarchy and politics to many believers due to past church experience. At the same time it doesn't get to the essence of why churches should band together. "Denomination" simply refers to "A recognized autonomous branch of a church or a religion."[3] But historic Christian denominations are more than that. They are a group of churches that confess the same doctrine and that have covenanted or "federated" together for the common good and the glory of God. Yet, "federation" connotes to many an overly-independent attitude that says, in effect, "No one can tell our church what to do."[4] But this should not be, as the very word "federation" comes from the Latin term *foedus*, or covenant. Federating churches affirm that they come together on the basis of their unity in faith and make mutual promises to each other as churches to work together.[5] Finally, the term "network" also seems insufficient to describe the relationship that kindred churches should share. A "network" is "an extended group of people with similar interests or concerns who interact and remain in informal contact for mutual assistance or support." It is probably the informality of networks that make them the most popular inter-church motif today. Our concern is that its informality is precisely the weak link in the system. As you can see, regardless of the terms' positives and negatives, our concern is with hierarchical tyranny on the one hand and absolute congregational autonomy on the other.

Preliminary Questions

One question that immediately arises when considering ecumenicity is, "How big a tent are we talking about?" The modern ecumenical movement seeks to draw together *everyone* who calls themselves Christian (or even religious). When *we* talk about ecumenical relations we are talking about relations among true churches of Christ (BC, art. 29) since being in a federative relationship must be founded on unity in faith and in confession. In biblical terms, "Do two walk together, unless they have agreed to meet?" (Amos 3:3).

Contrarily, we provoke the Lord to jealousy when we have fellowship in his name with those who do not follow his will (1 Corinthians 10:14–22). Paul makes clear that those who preach a false gospel are under the curse of God (Galatians 1:6–9). Naturally, churches that uphold the gospel cannot have fellowship with churches that do not. The true body of Christ is made up of Christian parts. We cannot incorporate non-Christian parts into the body (Ephesians 4:16–17).

A second question may be asked, especially among more independent-minded churches: "Is independent-ism unbiblical?" We'll be making the case that congregations should have federative relationships with other like-minded churches. This doesn't mean, however, that a church *cannot* exist independently, only that (in our estimation) it *should not* exist independently. It is of the well being (*bene esse*) of every local church to have fellowship with other churches. We are going to be arguing that independentism or congregationalism does not best fit the biblical paradigm nor best serve the churches on a practical level. At the same time, we disapprove of the tyranny that denominations sometimes exercise over their congregations, particularly in terms of their desire to depart.

Finally, a third question may come to mind: "Don't federations infringe on the *autonomy* of the local church?" We're going to be making the point that autonomy really isn't the best way to describe a local church. In an absolute sense, no church should be a law to itself. As well, we believe that when the decisions of denominational assemblies derive their authority from the Word of God they "are to be received with reverence and submission" (WCF, 31.3). Major assemblies (sometimes called Synods or General Assemblies, Classes or Presbyteries) do not have power or authority that is distinct in kind from the power that resides in the local church, but a power and authority that is distinct in degree. Both the local ruling body and the church assemblies have the authority of Christ, but the difference is that while the local elders have direct authority from Christ, the assemblies have indirect authority since they are made up of delegates from the local churches. As one writer says, "All church power is granted to officers through the call of Jesus Christ, which comes by the consent of the church. That is why local congregations nominate, call, and elect their own officers, both elders and deacons; no body is to be ruled by officers they do not choose for themselves."[6] In other words, the assemblies of multiple churches are not more authoritative because of their number. They are only as authoritative in so far as they take their stand upon Scripture. Hence the Protestant confession is that, "All synods or councils, since the Apostles' times, whether general or particular, may err; and many have erred" (WCF, 31.4). These assemblies only make decisions for those bodies duly represented by local church leaders.

Arguments in Favor of Federative Relationships

But is this whole idea of denominations, federations, or networks actually biblical? Haven't we in our day finally risen above the "modern" and schismatic notion of denominational affiliation? In answering these questions we should be clear that Scripture does not clearly prescribe all the details of a particular form of church government, and this is even more true in terms of denominational structure. Thus, as one twentieth-century writer on ecclesiology wrote, "Every form of church government has to wrestle with three important principles: The individual right of the believer, the representative character of the ministry under Christ and the unity of the Church.[7]" It is our conviction that the denominational structures of Reformed or Presbyterian government do the best job of balancing these three. In wrestling with these principles, four arguments seem to favor a presbyterian or presbyterial approach.[8] By "presbyterian" or "presbyterial" we mean that every local congregation is governed by a ruling body composed of a plurality of elders and that these elders form what is variously called a "consistory" or "session" that oversees the members of the congregation. We also mean that two or more consistories or sessions form a "classis" or "presbytery" (1 Timothy 4:14). Further, several classes or presbyteries form a "Synod" or "General Assembly" of churches. Besides what we will say below, we see this principle expressed in the division of the Old Testament church into escalating tiers of representation (Exodus 18:21–25). We recognize that in this example, Moses is at the top whereas in a federation model Christ is at the top, but it's the overall principle that we want to stress here: Among the people of God there is representation whether at the more narrow or more broad level.

First, there is the "body principle" that is highlighted throughout the New Testament, and especially in 1 Corinthians 12: "For just as the body is one and has many members, and all the members of the body, though many, are one body, so it is with Christ" (1 Corinthians 12:12). As individual Christians are part of the local church, the analogy can be extended to say that individual churches are part of the universal church of Christ. In other words, just as the distinct parts of the body are not disconnected from the body, so distinct churches do not stand disconnectedly alongside the larger church. To be a strictly independent church either in name or practice betrays a too small view of the church. "Each part of the church has a responsibility to the others and to the whole."[9] In reality, independent or nondenominational churches often function as a denomination unto themselves.

Second, the Bible shows significant interaction between churches. The early churches' pastors and elders joined together to make decisions that impacted the entire body of Christians throughout the world (Acts 15:1–35). Later, the Colossian and Thessalonian congregations were called upon to exchange the letters that they received from the apostle Paul for each other's mutual benefit (Colossians 4:16). Similarly, the seven churches in the book of Revelation were addressed as congregations in large urban centers that were joined together in their ministry. They each received a copy of John's apocalypse (Revelation 1:11, 20). Paul exhorted Titus to be concerned not only about his own congregation, but he was to appoint elders in the various cities on the island of Crete (Titus 1:5). Finally, Paul commended various congregations for their concern for their sister congregations by sending them financial contributions (2 Corinthians 8–9; Philippians 3).

Third, there is the argument of historical precedent. After the close of the New Testament canon the sort of church councils described in Acts 15 continued and still continue today, albeit, without the church's foundation-laying gift of the apostles. The first evidence of a primitive church council occurred in 150 AD. These sorts of meetings became common in the third century. And the decisions of these ecclesiastical assemblies were binding upon the churches represented.[10] From the fourth to the eighth centuries seven councils were held which are said to be ecumenical or general or universal. Therefore, it is the historic practice of local and regional churches to see themselves as unified tangibly by coming together for deliberation over serious matters.

Fourth, there is the obvious fact that individual congregations have inherent limitations. Just as on an individual level we need the spiritual gifts of others to offset our personal weaknesses, so on a congregational level we need the gifts of other congregations to offset our corporate weaknesses. Our individual vision is limited (1 Corinthians 13:9–10); that's one of the reasons we believe in having a plurality of elders. Churches that view the pastor as the only ruling elder easily get themselves in trouble. For this same reason we believe it is proper to federate with other churches. A congregation is limited by its background, geographical location, wisdom, and past experiences. But when congregations meet together they have another guard against their human imperfections and benefit from the wisdom of a multitude of counselors (Proverbs 11:14). A federation of churches are a check and balance to our sin nature as well as our myopic vision of the church.

Practical Expressions of Federative Relationships

In addition to these arguments in favor of federations based on the principles above, there are a number of practical benefits that can be attributed to fellowship in a denomination. Not the least of which is to deal with disagreement. Without broader assemblies, disagreements are less easily resolved. A biblical case in point is the Jerusalem Council (Acts 15). Paul and Barnabas were not able to resolve the conflict they had with the Judaizers, who were requiring Gentiles converts to Christ to adopt Jewish practices. Because of this Paul and Barnabas brought the matter before the apostles and elders at the request of the church at Antioch. The decisions of this Council were made applicable to the several churches involved in Syria and Asia Minor. The decisions made were not merely advisory but were to be received as binding.[11]

Second, federating churches facilitate fellowship between leaders and members. Most people regularly fellowship with their colleagues. Independent churches might find fewer opportunities to facilitate this kind of collegiality for their ministers and elders. Churches within federations are privileged to fellowship with fellow ministers who may visit from time to time.

Third, federating churches support each other financially (Romans 15:25–27). The first-century churches were so committed to a shared ministry that the congregations of Macedonia (e.g. Philippi, Thessalonica, and Berea) liberally supported Paul even while he worked among the believers in Corinth (2 Corinthians 8:1–5). One of the side effects of belonging to a federation is an increase in requests for help from financially needy congregations. But this is as it should be.

Fourth, federating churches promote the cause of missions. For example, the church in Antioch sent Paul and Barnabas to other parts of the world (Acts 13) while the church in Corinth assisted the church in Jerusalem (2 Corinthians 8–9).

Fifth, federating churches provide counsel: "Where there is no counsel, the people fall; but in the multitude of counselors there is wisdom" (Proverbs 11:14). We need to be corrected by others who use the Scripture for our benefit (1 Timothy 3:16–17). It should also go without saying that we should place the greatest value on the counsel of those who understand the Bible the way we do. The denomination in which we minister has a practice called "church visitation," where each church is visited regularly by officers from other churches for encouragement and accountability every two years.[12]

Don't take what we say the wrong way. Federative unions do not solve every problem. But we do believe that this Reformed vision reflects the Bible's teaching and serves churches well: "On the one hand it avoids the uncertainty of a pure democracy, as in independent polity; while, on the other hand, it avoids the despotism of the clergy, as in Episcopal polity. It is a form of government that is neither too widely diffused nor too narrowly concentrated."[13]

Questions

What is meant by the term "ecumenicity?"

How have ecumenical relationships been abused in our age?

What concerns could be raised over the practice of denominationalism?

What concerns could be raised over the practice of independentism?

Regardless of one's particular view of church government, provide some examples of how congregations in Scripture were related to each other in practical ways.

How does the "body principle" in 1 Corinthians 12 offer insights into inter-church relationships?

For Further Reading

J. De Jong, *Bound Yet Free: Readings in Reformed Church Polity* (Winnipeg: Premier Publishing, 1995).

William Heyns, *Handbook for Elders and Deacons: The Nature and the Duties of the Offices According to the Principles of Reformed Church Polity* (Grand Rapids: Wm. B. Eerdmans Publishing Company, 1928), 41–48.

J. L. Schaver, *The Polity of the Churches, Volume 1: Concerns All the Churches of Christendom* (Chicago: Church Polity Press, 1947), 79–107.

Chapter Five

Outside of a Denomination

I was totally new to this whole "Reformed" thing so I decided to pick up the phone and call a Reformed church near where I lived to talk to a pastor. The phone rang and he answered, "(City) Church." I thought maybe I had made a mistake because I was calling the (City) Reformed Church but he didn't include "Reformed" in his greeting. One of the things I learned from our ensuing conversation was that he believed his was the only "true" church in the area; everyone else was not really a church.

How do you view your congregation? Do you think in Elijah's terms, "I, even I only, am left?" (1 Kings 19:10) Few of us view the church landscape with quite as much despair as Elijah did during the days of King Ahab. Yet many of us have a tendency to disparage the way that others serve the Lord or forget they exist altogether. Elijah had essentially become a denomination of one. God gently reproved his exclusivism by reminding him that there were seven thousand others in Israel, all of whose knees had not bowed to Baal (1 Kings 19:18). These "other" worshipers of the Lord have been preserved by the Lord himself. The Lord graciously reminded Elijah to be significantly more ecumenical than he was prone to being. In doing so he speaks to us as well.

The topic of ecumenicity, or the practice of demonstrating the connectedness of the universal church, closely relates to the other three components of a vibrant church that are considered in this book. First, under the heading of identity (part 1), we said that the church is a possession of Christ. The supremacy of Christ over the church has profound implications for how we relate to other churches. Second, under the heading of authority (part 2), we learned that Christ cares for the church through officers of his choosing. The leaders of the church are responsible for taking the initiative in promoting cooperation with other churches as much as is biblically and practically possible. Finally, the church's activity (part 4) also relates to the church's ecumenicity. Our churches should carefully consider how we might engage in our mission in concert with other churches of Christ, especially with other local churches.

In the last chapter we thought about ecumenicity within a denomination. We now consider ecumenicity beyond the bounds of one's own denomination or federation.

The Need for Biblical Ecumenism

For people who are accustomed to independent or non-denominational churches, the need to demonstrate fellowship with other local churches may not be apparent. But the Bible does present a clear mandate for a proper ecumenism.

In John 17 Jesus prayed for all those who would believe in him through the words of the apostles. The essence of his prayer is "that they all may be one" (John 17:20). Jesus compares the unity of the church with the unity that exists between the Father and the Son; therefore his people should be one "just as you, Father, are in me, and I in you" (John 17:21). He is teaching that the unity of Christians is to be a reflection of the unity of the Godhead. After all, if the church represents the visible ministry of God on earth, this is what people will see. That's why Jesus says that through

Christian unity "the world may believe that [the Father] sent [the Son]" (John 17:21). The church is commanded to be a unified, loving community in order to present a united front to the world.

Some will object that this unity is demonstrated merely by the invisible church or the spiritual body of Christ. Of course it is true that everyone who is united to Christ by a living faith does dwell in perfect spiritual union with each other as well. But this fact is so obvious that Jesus would not have to pray for it. The spiritual union of the invisible church is assumed. As Berkhof said, "But this invisible church naturally takes a visible form."[1] Visible, local congregations of Jesus Christ are charged to demonstrate practically union with other churches similarly bought by the blood of Christ.

This point is clarified by Ephesians 4. There Paul wrote of the unity of the church saying, "There is one body and one Spirit—just as you were called to the one hope that belongs to your call—one Lord, one faith, one baptism, one God and Father of all, who is over all and through all and in all" (Ephesians 4:4–6). Paul isn't just expressing a theological fact. He is giving an exhortation. Believers are urged to "walk in a manner worthy of the calling to which you have been called, with all humility and gentleness, with patience, bearing with one another in love, eager to maintain the unity of the Spirit in the bond of peace" (Ephesians 4:1–3). Paul is saying we are not simply to confess the catholicity (or universality) of the church theologically but to walk in it practically. Through the mutual edification such a relationship between congregations can bring and the witness this gives to the world, one denomination alongside of another manifests their spiritual unity.[2]

In addition to this biblical data, there are practical reasons for congregations to maintain positive contact and cooperation with others. As churches continue to do their own thing the church is perceived by the world as schismatic. Effectiveness is reduced.

Churches and believers become imbalanced. Ecumenicity is not just an idealistic vision; but a duty impressed upon the churches of Christ. Nonetheless there remain significant roadblocks to biblical ecumenicity, which we will explain below.

The Roadblocks to Biblical Ecumenism

The first roadblock to biblical ecumenism is a failure to differentiate modern ecumenism with its biblical counterpart. There is a push today to combine all religious expressions under one roof, thus leveling all theological distinctions and creating a "lowest-common-denominator" Christianity. We should rightly reject such an approach. But we shouldn't throw the baby out with the bathwater. We are simply saying that the true church is bigger than our congregation, than our denominations, and than our particular theological heritages. Our practice of ecumenicity should reflect this principle.

Another roadblock to biblical ecumenism is a too-narrow definition of the true church. Sometimes we assume that a very narrow understanding of the true church is required by our particular traditions and confessions. I once read a pamphlet by a denomination that said in effect, "We're not saying we're the only true church; we're just not aware of anyone else." But upon closer inspection, our traditions may not call for such a narrow view of the true church as we had previously suspected. For example, scholars have described sixteenth and seventeenth-century Reformed churches as "international Calvinism." From Hungary in the east to England in the west, the Reformed churches recognized each other as true and faithful churches despite differences of a secondary nature. As John Calvin said in 1552 of the prospect of an international Reformed Synod because of the struggles facing the church: "So much does this concern me, that, could I be of any service, I would not grudge to cross even ten seas, if need were, on account of it."[3]

Calvin certainly has a reputation for being narrow-minded and exclusivistic. Yet, when writing on the comparison between the false church and the true he said, "... trivial errors in this ministry ought not to make us regard it as illegitimate." What did Calvin mean by "trivial errors?" He explained: "... the errors to which such pardon is due, are those by which the fundamental doctrine of religion is not injured, and by which those articles of religion, in which all believers should agree, are not suppressed, while, in regard to the sacraments, the defects are such as neither destroy nor impair the legitimate institution of their Author." Clearly Calvin did not have in mind the sort of differences that often divide the church today. He had in mind bigger issues, as he went on to explain: "But as soon as falsehood has forced its way into the citadel of religion, as soon as the sum of necessary doctrine is inverted, and the use of the sacraments is destroyed, the death of the Church undoubtedly ensues."[4]

Confusion relating to our understanding of the true and false church can also be traced to misunderstandings related to one of the early reformed statements of faith, the Belgic Confession. The Belgic Confession speaks of the marks of the true church as the pure preaching of the gospel, and pure administration of the sacraments, and the exercise of church discipline (BC, art. 29). We wholeheartedly agree. But we are also convinced that these marks are misapplied when used to say that certain Bible-believing, Christ-exalting evangelical churches are false churches. The Belgic Confession clearly has Roman Catholicism in its scopes when it distinguishes between the true and *the* false church. The marks it gives were meant to show that *this* "church," was a false church.[5] The Confession summarizes its three marks by saying, "in short, if all things are managed according to the pure Word of God, all things contrary thereto rejected, and Jesus Christ acknowledged as the only Head of the Church" (BC, art. 29).[6] The Belgic Confession acknowledges that in true Christians there remain "great infirmities." The same is true with regard to true Christian churches.[7]

Another closely related sixteenth century confession helps clarify our point. The Second Helvetic Confession (1566) helps us understand that we ought not be surprised to find problems and multiformity among true Christian churches:

> ... we do not so strictly shut up the church within those marks ... as thereby to exclude all those out of the church which either do not communicate in the sacraments (not willingly, nor upon contempt, but who, being constrained by necessity, against their will abstain from them, or else do want them); or in whom faith sometimes fails, though not quite decay, nor altogether die: or in whom some slips and errors of infirmity may be found. For we know that God had some friends in the world that were not of the commonwealth of Israel. We know what befell the people of God in the captivity of Babylon, where they wanted their sacrifices seventy years. We know what happened to St. Peter, who denied his Master, and what is wont daily to fall out among the faithful and chosen of God, which go astray and are full of infirmities. We know moreover, what manner of churches the churches at Galatia and Corinth were in the apostles' times: in which the apostle condemns divers great and heinous crimes; yet he calls them holy churches of Christ (1 Corinthians 1:2; Galatians 1:2) ...

> ... the truth and unity of the church consists ... not in outward rites and ceremonies, but rather in the truth and unity of the catholic faith. This catholic faith is not taught us by the ordinances or laws of men, but by the Holy Scriptures, a compendious and short sum whereof is the Apostles' Creed. And, therefore, we read in the ancient writers that there were manifold diversities of ceremonies, but that those were always free; neither did any man think that the unity of the church was thereby broken or dissolved. (Ch. 17)[8]

Further clarification is provided in the seventeenth-century Westminster Confession of Faith:

> This Catholic (or universal) church has been sometimes more, sometimes less visible. And particular Churches, which are members thereof, are more or less pure, according as the doctrine of the gospel is taught and embraced, ordinances administered, and public worship performed more or less purely in them. The purest Churches under heaven are subject both to mixture and error. (WCF, 25:4, 5)

A final roadblock to biblical ecumenism is the mistaken notion that we have nothing to give or share with churches that are different than ours. One of the ministries of the Spirit is to promote fellowship (*koinonia*). This fellowship exists when two parties, being united by some common bond, give and receive freely together. If we have something that other believers can benefit from we must share it. We should also admit that other believers have things that we need. Some churches excel in joyfulness, others in sobriety. Some have made greater strides in evangelism, others in biblical scholarship and study habits. Until the church reaches "mature manhood" (Ephesians 4:13) at the coming of the Lord, there will always be opportunity to give and share amongst itself.

The Expression of Biblical Ecumenism
If the need for practical unity among Christian congregations has been granted and the roadblocks overcome, the question still remains, "What does biblical ecumenism look like?" We need to answer this question to avoid idyllic and unrealistic expectations of what we can expect to happen between churches of varying church governments, histories, and theological expression. On the other hand, without a clear sense of what we should be striving for we will likely not gain much ground toward the biblical ideal for inter-church fellowship.

The first thing local churches need to do is establish a standard for fellowship. There are small and great errors within the church. These errors will dictate to what level we may have fellowship with various manifestations of the church. We are compelled to demonstrate some form of fellowship with true churches and to abstain from fellowship with false churches. In this sense, doctrine must both divide and unite. The doctrines of the Scriptures are the dividing line between those who have God and those who do not (2 John 9). Our conviction is that local congregations ought to develop a relationship with other congregations who demonstrate a commitment to the gospel and "to the Bible in its entirety as the Word of God, written, without errors in all its parts ..."[9] Such churches will conform to exegetically reasonable positions that differ from other churches that are committed to Scripture. A few years ago, I was asked on the steps of our church building whether I considered Baptists to be Christian. I was embarrassed by the question. Still, these kinds of questions need to be answered if we have any hope of developing relationships with Christians outside of our immediate ecclesiastical enclave.

A closely related step in developing inter-church relationships is to exercise a judgment of charity. Again, the Second Helvetic Confession speaks to this: "We are to have a special regard that we judge not rashly before the time, nor go about to exclude and cast off or cut away those whom the Lord would not have excluded nor cut off, or whom, without some damage to the church, we cannot separate from it" (Ch. 17).[10] This comment is made with regard to church members but there is a close connection to the church as a whole. This section ends with a reference to Philippians 3:15–16: "Let those of us who are mature think this way, and if in anything you think otherwise, God will reveal that also to you. Only let us hold true to what we have attained."

Third, in developing a biblical ecumenicity, begin with churches closest to us theologically and geographically.[11] When it comes to marriage we should be wary of the adage, "Opposites attract." This may be true in terms of personalities and casual interests but a couple that enters a marriage with disharmonious theological convictions can expect to face serious difficulties in their walk together. The same can be said of churches. Realistically, we should expend our greatest collective energies with those whom we are most closely aligned. On the other hand, two Bible-believing, Christ-exalting churches across the street or around the corner from each other should work at developing a loving, and mutually edifying relationship with each other regardless of denominational affiliation or cultural-religious heritage.

Fourth, Christian churches need to develop real relationships with like-minded churches. They must engage on those issues and problems that divide them as well as on those that they face in common. They should strive to share insights and, "communicate advantages to one another."[12] As individuals we should encourage believers from congregations other than ours. We may have significant differences with them; we shouldn't shy away from graciously discussing these differences. Indeed, as the Second Helvetic Confession says, "It pleases God to use the dissensions that arise in the church to the glory of His Name, to the setting forth of the truth" (Ch. 17).[13] But we should be cautious of unconstructively criticizing other churches or theological traditions. Along these lines, congregations that have experienced schism and conflict with others should work diligently to restore broken relationships. The split that took place between Paul and Barnabas (and John Mark) was regrettable (Acts 15:16–40). But we are encouraged by the fact that later on the breach was mended between these brothers.[14]

Finally, churches in ecumenical relation with each other should assist each other in the promotion of biblical faith. Areas to explore here include cooperation in missions, relief efforts, Christian schools, and various areas of biblical and theological education such as in the training of officer-bearers. Pulpit exchanges between ministers not only provide a greater variety to the ministry, they can also help strengthen the bond between the participating congregations. Local conferences featuring practical, biblical, expository or historical messages by gifted local teachers can help bring area believers together as well as showcase the beauty of the biblical faith to those who might presently attend false or "less pure" churches.

In the end, the Heidelberg Catechism expresses ecumenicity so beautifully when it says we believe, "That out of the whole human race, from the beginning to the end of the world, the Son of God, by His Spirit and Word, gathers, defends, and preserves for Himself unto everlasting life a chosen communion in the unity of the true faith" (HC, Q&A 54), and that members of this church are therefore "bound to use [their] gifts readily and cheerfully for the advantage and welfare of other members" (HC, Q&A 55).

Questions

How is biblical ecumenicity stressed or exemplified in your congregation?

What danger exists in too narrowly identifying true churches?

What danger exists in too broadly identifying true churches?

What sort of relationships do evangelical churches in your community have?

What are some solid churches in your area that are not in your federation/denomination? Have you established any sort of fellowship with them? Why or why not?

Can you suggest other ways in which Christian churches can demonstrate their unity in Christ?

For Further Reading
www.naparc.org

W. Robert Godfrey, "A Reformed Dream." (http://www.modernreformation.org)

Daniel R. Hyde, "From Reformed Dream to Reformed Reality: The Problem and Possibility of Reformed Church Unity." (http://theaquilareport.com)

Part Four

Activity

Chapter Six

A Teaching Church

The Bible is the Word of God. All Bible-believing evangelical churches affirm this. But why, then, don't all practice it? This was what led me as a new believer within Pentecostalism to search for a theology that put its money where its mouth was. What I found was the theology of the Word from the Protestant Reformation, which not only professed *sola Scriptura* against the Roman Church but also professed the sufficiency of Scripture for all things concerning doctrine, worship, and godliness. I was struck by how little Scripture reading and exposition there was in the church circles I was used to as compared to the first Reformed church I walked into. In my new church there was an Old Testament reading, a New Testament reading, a prayer for illumination, and a lengthy sermon. It was obvious to me that preaching the Word was central.

Throughout this book we have been considering the principles that form the foundation of a well-ordered church that will find its identity in Christ alone, will follow the Bible's plan for authority in the form of pastors, elders, and deacons, and will engage in ecumenicity in a healthy and responsible way. In this final part we see that a well-ordered church will have a clear sense of its activity and will strive, with God's help, to fulfill this mission. We're using "mission" here not in the narrow sense of missionary activity, but in the general sense of "an operational task." What is the task of the church? This question is important not only for the leaders of a well-ordered church, but also for the members. Since the church is described in Scripture as a body—a living organism—every member will be involved in some way in the church's mission. We will highlight four essential aspects of the activity or mission of the local church: A well-ordered church is a teaching church, a worshiping church, a witnessing church, and a repenting church.

In a sense, the most basic of these tasks is that of teaching. Without a robust, biblical teaching ministry a church may fail to grasp the implications of its identity in Christ, may fail to understand God's plan for its authority, and may fail to engage in ecumenicity. Likewise, apart from plain, powerful Bible teaching the church will be ill equipped to fulfill its activity of worshiping, witnessing, and repenting. As the leadership of the church is increasingly being pulled in many directions, we need to be reminded of the need for the church to focus on teaching.

The Need to be a Teaching Church

The New Testament church, as the "pillar and buttress of the truth" (1 Timothy 3:15), inherited a rich teaching tradition from the Old Testament people of God. Because the Levites failed in their responsibility to teach the people as they were called to do (Deuteronomy 31:9–13), God raised up prophets to proclaim his Word. The central tasks of the prophets was to pray for the people and to teach the people "… the statutes and the laws, and make them know the way in which they must walk and what they must do" (Exodus 18:20). In fact, the Apostle Paul summarizes the Old Testament dispensation as a time of the law being a rigorous teacher (Galatians 3:24).

At the coming of Christ, divine instruction took on flesh and blood. We see a common picture in the gospels: "… and crowds gathered to him again, And again, as was his custom, he taught them" (Mark 10:1; cf. Matthew 4:23–25). Jesus focused so much on teaching because as the Christ, he summed up in himself not only the Old Testament offices of priest and king, but also prophet. He was "ordained of God the Father and anointed with the Holy Ghost to be our chief Prophet and Teacher, who has fully revealed to us the secret counsel and will of God concerning our redemption" (HC, Q&A 31).[1] The "Good Teacher," has left a lofty standard for teaching in the church.

God's emphasis on teaching is further highlighted by the various lists of spiritual gifts in the New Testament which focus on teaching. The Bible describes the gift of spiritual discernment (1 Corinthians 12:10), or a perception in judging spiritual things. This teaching gift is so important because not all of us have good discernment. Consider the example of Jethro, who began by asking questions. Then he offered his spiritual judgment in clear terms by proposing an alternate plan for Moses (Exodus 18:14ff.). As the Proverbs would later say, "The purpose in a man's heart is like deep water, but a man of understanding will draw it out" (Proverbs 20:5). Then there is the gift of "a word of knowledge" (1 Corinthians 12:8). Knowledge refers to an awareness of and ability to articulate sacred things. Paul also writes of the gift of prophecy (Romans 12:6, 1 Corinthians 12:28) which should probably be distinguished from the office of a prophet. Paul seems to be speaking of ministers as giving prophetic utterance (1 Corinthians 14:1–5). All the "gifts" Paul speaks of in Ephesians 4 are those of the ministry of the Word: apostles, prophets, evangelists, shepherds, and teachers (Ephesians 4:11). Finally, teaching is described as exhortation (Romans 12:8) or applying doctrine to the hearts of the hearers, to their consciences and feelings. The fact that so many of the spiritual gifts are teaching oriented underlines the need for teaching churches today.

In his book, *City on a Hill*, Phillip Ryken asserts that, "A Church for post-Christian times is a teaching church." He goes on to say that "the only church that will survive in post-Christian times is a church with a passion for God's Word."[2] Especially as truth is questioned it will be increasingly necessary for us to clearly articulate what God has said in his Word. It will also become increasingly necessary to deny the teachings presented under the guise of Christianity, which God has not taught in his Word.

What Does a Teaching Church Look Like?
There are several discernable marks of a teaching church. These marks have implications for both the leadership and the members of the congregation.

A Teaching Church Is Led By an Equipped Minister
Much is made today of the fact that formal theological seminary training is not required in Scripture. Obviously there is no command requiring institutions that mirror contemporary seminaries. But certainly the New Testament writers assume *equivalent* training to prepare one for the ministry. Ministerial training that resembles the New Testament paradigm will combine inter-personal discipleship, heart-warming devotion, and academic discipline.[3]

One of the problems with seminary education in many cases today is that it is extracted from discipleship in the church. Modern critics of seminaries see them as "spiritual information factories" that do not prepare men for real-life ministry in the church. Paul charged Timothy: "what you have heard from me in the presence of many witnesses entrust to faithful men who will be able to teach others also" (2 Timothy 2:2). Churches today need to lead their men through seminary by not only providing for them financially but also seeing that they are discipled by coming along side of more seasoned ministers.

If seminaries are to properly prepare men for ministry today they must also seek to inculcate in their students a living piety. In the book of Acts, Luke makes a remarkable statement. He says that the Pharisees could observe that the disciples had been with Jesus (Acts 4:13). The Pharisees perception of them as uneducated and merely common men was inaccurate. True, they didn't have the same credentials as the scribes and teachers of the law but they had been nurtured in the seedbed (Latin, *seminarium*) of the gospel in the care of the Master Gardener. They had studied with him, asked questions of him, been corrected by him and grown in their love for him. They were scorned for their lack of intellectual decorum. But during their three years of "seminary training" they grew to love their Lord with all their heart, soul, mind and strength (Mark 12:30).

As important as seminary (or something like it) is, it is not enough. God's teachers need continued training. For example, during the sixteenth and seventeenth centuries, the Reformed churches were known for an activity known as "prophesyings." At these gatherings of ministers, each man would take a turn preaching and then being critiqued, as a means of continual growth in competence. Much ministerial training results from diligent "on-the-job" faithfulness. A minister must be a diligent worker who is given the freedom to spend time "rightly handling the word of truth" (2 Timothy 2:14–16). Paul wrote to Timothy, "Keep a close watch on yourself and on the teaching. Persist in this, for by so doing you will save both yourself and your hearers" (1 Timothy 4:16; cf. 2 Timothy 3:14; 4:1–5). Such continued training will include reading, speaking at events (other than local worship services) and attending conferences.[4]

A Teaching Church Provides Ample Time for Teaching
Historically, Christian congregations had at least two worship services on the Lord's Day.[5] One reason for this phenomenon is expressed in the Heidelberg Catechism's explanation of the

Sabbath command: "that I, especially on the day of rest, diligently attend church to learn the Word of God" (HC, Q&A 103).[6] Sunday schools, mid-week classes, and small groups can certainly provide additional teaching and fellowship time. But God's primary means of conveying, not merely information, but grace itself, is the preaching of the Word (Acts 2:42; Romans 10:17). For this reason a teaching church will see the sermon as the centerpiece of the worship service(s).

Extraordinarily lengthy sermons are not necessarily a tell-tale sign of a teaching church. In fact, there is no excuse for prolixity or pointless meandering on the part of the minister. But it is a bad sign when church members are more concerned about the length of the sermon than its contents. For example, I once preached a thirty minute sermon as a guest preacher in a neighboring congregation. After the service I commented on the beautiful early spring weather, "You hardly need a coat," I remarked. As I turned toward my car one of the members responded just loudly enough to hear, "He may not need a coat but he does need a wrist-watch!" It is important to ask ourselves as leaders in Christ's church, "How much time does our church spend in teaching compared with other areas?"

A Teaching Church Understands Teaching Not Merely as Informing but as Equipping

The modern disdain for preaching seems to stem, in part, from the fact that some preaching is indistinguishable from lecturing. Academic lecturing from church pulpits is surely one of the reasons that J. I. Packer can say, "Most churches today have passengers rather than practitioners."[7]

If Scripture is useful for doctrine, reproof, correction, and instruction in righteousness, then teachers should use it in that way "that the man of God may be complete, equipped for every good work (2 Timothy 3:17). The Presbyterian Church in America's

Book of Church Order refers to the teaching duty of the church as discipline or systematic training under the authority of God's Scripture.[8] In the classic passage on the equipping ministry of the church, Ephesians 4:11–16, we get a clear picture of the relationship between the teaching ministry and the collective ministry of the church: the pastor-teachers are to equip the saints for the works of ministry.[9] The equipping of the saints must also take place in personal, one-on-one interactions. But much can be accomplished, with God's help, through biblical sermons that not only scrutinize the text using the traditional questions, "who, what, when, where, and why," but that also practically assist the listener by explaining the "how." Sermons must explain the "what" of the text as well as the "so what." Doctrine must lead to what the Puritans called "use," also known as application. A. W. Tozer was right: "Exposition must have application."[10] Application is a biblical must of preaching. The application portion of the sermon is not the opportunity for the preacher to bring up his "hobby horses," but to faithfully and lovingly draw out the significance of the text in terms of how God's people must respond to it.

A Teaching Church Is Committed to Being a Learning Church

If there are teaching duties of a well-ordered church there are also learning duties that are shared by each of the members. In the form for the public profession of faith in the denomination in which we serve the minister gives this charge to the prospective new members: "I charge you, then, beloved, that you, *by the diligent use of the means of grace* and with the assistance of your God, continue in the profession which you have just made."[11] Later in the prayer, the minister prays that God will "increase them in the spirit of wisdom and understanding, the spirit of counsel and might, the spirit of knowledge and the fear of the Lord."[12] Church membership vows oblige us to be students in a learning church.

The "means of grace" in the above quotation are especially the preached Word and the sacraments of baptism and the Lord's

Supper. It's amazing that so much emphasis today is placed on private Bible reading as means of knowing God and his will, while relatively little stress is placed on the obligation of each member of Christ to diligently and regularly attend to the preached Word. As we read the Word, but especially as we hear it proclaimed, God speaks his Word about the work of his Son through the helping ministry of the Holy Spirit. This Word is directed to the head, hearts, and hands of sinners for one very important purpose; that we would increasingly turn from our sins and to God. That's why the preached Word is the heartbeat of the Christian ministry and of the Christian life. Private Bible reading is not enough. In fact, it could indicate a smugness and an unwillingness to be taught in the church.

The Westminster Larger Catechism outlines some of the duties placed upon those who hear the Word preached:

> It is required of those that hear the word preached that they attend upon it with diligence, preparation and prayer; examine what they hear by the Scriptures; receive the truth with faith, love, meekness, and readiness of mind, as the Word of God; mediate, and confer of it; hide it in their hearts, and bring forth the fruit of it in their lives. (WLC, Q&A 160)[13]

A learning church, then, should encourage people to bring their Bibles to church, to mark them up, to take notes, and to ask questions when appropriate.

A Teaching Church Expects All Its Members to Teach

Not everyone in the church is called to be a teacher in the proper sense. But we all have opportunities to exhort (Romans 15:14). We would love nothing more than to have people from our congregations volunteer to teach something: a financial class, a marriage study, a youth group meeting—the possibilities are endless. The teaching obligation of the church is manifested in a special way in the home. God solemnly charged his people: "You shall teach [the words of God] to your children, talking of them when you are sitting in your house, and when you are walking by the way, and when you lie down, and when you rise" (Deuteronomy 11:19). The church exercises its teaching ministry by equipping families in the covenant communities to be teaching and learning communities under the leadership of the heads of households.

Attributes of Effective Teaching

As we think about what it means to be a teaching church, we believe there are several attributes that make up an effective teaching ministry of the Word of God.

First, it will be rooted in the theology found in Scripture and particularly Scripture's doctrine of God. Our strength and encouragement comes from knowing who God is, what he has done, what he is doing, and what he will do.

Second, it will be engaging. If we actually have something to say from God, we should say it in a way that people will actually hear. Jesus told stories, used colorful words, employed irony, and wasn't afraid to use shock value.

Third, it will be authoritative: "Thus says the Lord." We must echo God's words with confidence. When God's Word speaks, we must speak; when God's Word is silent, we must be silent.

Fourth, it must be comprehensive, embracing the "whole counsel of God" (Acts 20:27). One of the benefits of expository preaching (verse-by-verse, chapter-by-chapter teaching of Scripture) is that even difficult issues must be addressed as they come up in Scripture.

Fifth, it must be filled with exhortation (Romans 12:8), applying doctrine to the heart. A significant question that a Christian ministry must constantly be asking is "How can our people use this information?"[14]

Sixth, it must be intelligible to a wide variety of people both inside the church as well as those who come from outside, to adults and to children. Our motto should be "Scholarly in the study, simple in the pulpit (or at the lectern)."

Seventh, it must be nourishing to the soul. Teaching should feed the sheep (John 21:15–17) and thus administer spiritual health. Teaching should be loving and edifying and not needlessly controversial.

Eighth, it must be Christ-centered. If our teaching doesn't get to Christ—our need for him and his provision for us—then it is less than Christian. Without the gospel we have nothing to say. Because of the gospel we have every reason to be a teaching church.

Questions

What are some of the things that compete for the place of teaching in the church?

How can you evaluate how seriously you *personally* take the teaching ministry of the church?

Reflect on Acts 4:13. How could the Pharisees tell that Peter and John had been with Jesus?

How can Pastors and other educators strive to make instruction winsome?

Why is important to teach "the whole counsel of God"? How can we do this?

How can you assist your pastor in his teaching ministry?

For Further Reading

William Boekestein, "Profiting from Preaching: Learning to Truly Hear God" *The Outlook* 64:4 (2014): 22–24.

William Boekestein, "A Model Sermon." (http://www. reformation21.org/articles/a-model-sermon.php)

Wayne Mack and Dave Swaely, *Life in the Father's House: A Member's Guide to the Local Church* (Phillipsburg: P&R Publishing, 2006).

T. David Gordon, *Why Johnny Can't Preach: The Media Have Shaped the Messengers* (Phillipsburg, NJ: P&R Publishing, 2009).

Chapter Seven

A Worshiping Church

"What we need is some good old fashioned Pentecostal worship," the campus pastor exhorted my fellow students in a college chapel. It was about this time that I was coming to the realization that the issue of worship was so important to all Christian traditions. I was baptized into the Roman Catholic Church, spent a couple of years in my early childhood in the Calvary Chapel movement after my dad was converted, was converted myself in a Foursquare Church years later, went to an Assemblies of God college, and while there, was becoming more and more Reformed in my theology. It was becoming abundantly clear to me that the theology and practice of worship actually matter.

Worship is the goal of the church's mission. In fulfilling its activity of teaching, the church seeks to bring salvation to the lost and sanctification to the saved, to reach the lost and then to teach the reached. And all this is for the purpose of worshiping the Triune God who saves.

There are at least four key components of biblical worship with which a church's leadership especially, but all the people of God, need to be familiar. First, the basis for our worship is God's calling and redeeming us. Second, the object of our worship is the Triune God of grace who has accomplished and applied redemption. Third, the means by which we engage in our worship is the authoritative and sufficient Word of God. Fourth, the practice of our worship—all the details of what worship actually looks like—really matters (chapter 8).

The Basis for Worship

In discussing the basis for worship we are seeking to answer the question, "Why worship?" The answer goes back to what we covered at the very beginning of this book in terms of our identity as churches of Christ. We worship because of who God has made us to be in Jesus Christ, namely, the chosen and redeemed people of God. From before the foundation of the world he has chosen us to be his holy and blameless people (Ephesians 1:4). He has brought us into his family by delivering his people from the bondage and punishment of sin by the precious blood of Jesus Christ (Galatians 3:13; 4:5).

What do election and redemption have to do with worship? Sometimes the idea of God's sovereign electing choice is misunderstood as not having a purpose or goal. But if God has chosen you it is not so that you can rest contentedly and live for your own purpose. The Bible says that God has chosen his people to worship him (Psalm 100:1–3). Election leads to action. Jesus Christ is the "chosen and precious" living foundational stone of the church (1 Peter 2:4). Because we are connected to him, we too are living stones that God is building "as a spiritual house, to be a holy priesthood, to offer spiritual sacrifices acceptable to God through Jesus Christ" (1 Peter 2:5). And in contrast to those who reject Christ, Peter goes on to say, "But you are a chosen race, a royal priesthood, a holy nation, a people for his own possession" for the purpose of "proclaim[ing] the excellencies of him who called you out of darkness into his marvelous light" (1 Peter 2:9). In similar fashion, Israel was called out of Egypt to worship the Lord at Mount Sinai. (Exodus 3:12; cf. Exodus 19:6). Paul also connects our calling with our purpose of worshiping: "But we ought always to give thanks to God for you, brothers beloved by the Lord, because God chose you as the firstfruits to be saved, through sanctification by the Spirit and belief in the truth" (2 Thessalonians 2:13). In a word, all the biblical doctrines of election, redemption, sanctification, and glorification end in the worship of the God who elects, redeems, sanctifies, and glorifies.

For example, far from being a useless and speculative doctrine, election in Christ is a driving force of our worship. One seventeenth century pastor, Wilhelmus à Brakel (1635–1711), explained: "When the godly perceive that the beginning, middle, end [of their salvation], yes, everything proceeds only from God according to his eternal election ... it will then stir up the soul to return everything to God and in all things to honor and glorify Him, most heartily thanking him." He went on to say that when the godly reflect on God's sovereign election they will lose themselves in "sweet amazement only to arise afterwards to worship, be at rest, and rejoice that God's glory so far exceeds his comprehension."[1] The Reformed confessional statement, the Canons of Dort (1618–19), says this about the relationship between election and worship:

> The sense and certainty of this election afford to the children of God additional matter for daily humiliation before Him, for adoring the depth of His mercies, for cleansing themselves, and rendering grateful returns of ardent love to Him who first manifested so great love towards them. The consideration of this doctrine of election is so far from encouraging remissness in the observance of the divine commands or from sinking men in carnal security, that these, in the just judgment of God, are the usual effects of rash presumption or of idle and wanton trifling with the

grace of election, in those who refuse to walk in the ways of the elect (CD 1.13).[2]

When you know that it was God who chose you of all people, this can lead to only one place: adoration. In the words of John Calvin, believers should be in daily meditation on the fact that "all God's blessings with which he favors us are intended for this end, that his glory might be proclaimed by us."[3]

The Object of Worship

So God's works are the basis of worship. The obvious reflex on our part is that he alone is the object of our worship. As Jesus said, true worshipers worship "the Father" (John 4:23). Right worship of God, said Calvin, is "to ascribe and render to Him the glory of all that is good, to seek all things in Him alone, and in every want have recourse to Him alone."[4] True worship is, in a manner of speaking, to have a "God-complex."

More specifically, we worship the Triune God—Father, Son, and Holy Spirit. Scripture helps us by saying that we worship the Father, through the Son, in the power and fellowship of the Holy Spirit. As Paul says, "For through him"—Jesus Christ—"we both have access in one Spirit to the Father" (Ephesians 2:18). As Peter says, "You yourselves like living stones are being built up as a spiritual house, to be a holy priesthood, to offer spiritual sacrifices acceptable to God through Jesus Christ" (1 Peter 2:5). "Spiritual" sacrifices are those sacrifices the Holy Spirit leads us to offer in reliance upon him.

But we may miss the implications of the obvious fact that true worship finds its center in God. The God-centeredness of true Christian worship teaches us something very fundamental about our worship services. In the words of Robert Rayburn,

Good worship services are not for the enjoyment of the

worshipers. They are to provide an opportunity for devout believers to offer the sovereign God of the universe that adoration, praise, honor, and submission of which He is worthy and to receive that spiritual food which He provides true worshipers only through the Word and the sacraments.[5]

Worship is not for spectators to watch but for worshipers to participate in by glorifying God and by receiving grace as they sit at Jesus' feet. As soon as we forget this we are headed for trouble.

Worship is not the church's gift to the worshipers but the worshiper's gift to God (Psalm 116:12–13). Does your church come to worship to give glory and honor to God? As we wrestle with this question we should ask other diagnostic questions. For example, "What does our singing, our timeliness, our giving suggest about the direction of our worship?" On a corporate level we should ask, "Are our services chiefly aimed at attracting people? Are we focused on having just the right instruments or just the right praise leader?" We need to be careful that the direction of our worship doesn't start drooping horizontally. This is not to reject a model of worship that is sensitive to the understandings of those assembled. It is simply to get the seeker right: "true worshipers will worship the Father in spirit and truth, for the Father is seeking such people to worship him" (John 4:23).

The Means of Worship

When it comes to understanding the principles that rightly order our worship of the Triune God, we must think rightly about the means God has given us: the Word. The Word is God's all-sufficient source of communicating himself to the world. As we come to understand that the Word is sufficient we begin to see that it is all we need for what we believe about him (theology), for how we are to live for him (piety) and for how we are to worship him (liturgy).

In thinking about the Word's relationship to worship, we need to organize the principles of the Word into two groups. In John 4:24 Jesus sets forth two basic principles that govern worship. He says that true worshipers worship in "spirit" and in "truth." There is some discussion about exactly what these two terms mean but it seems safe to say that the first is more subjective or internal with respect to the worshiper and the second is more objective or external to the worshiper. In other words, when thinking about worship we need to understand, first, the heart matters of worship—the spirit of the matter—and second, that Scripture must regulate, the truth of the matter. If we miss either of these two fundamental principles our worship will degenerate either into sentimentalism (if it is not regulated by Scripture) or ceremonialism (if it is not sincerely expressed from the heart).

Scripture Regulates

Jesus said that true worship is "in truth." That is, true worship is governed by the truth of the Word. The sixteenth century reformers developed this principle from Scripture to help the church sort through the questions many people were asking about the worship in the Roman church. John Calvin, for example, draws this principle of Word-governed worship from the second commandment. If the first commandment (against the worship of other gods) specifies *which* God must be worshiped, the second (against image worship) specifies *how* this one true God must be worshipped. In particular, worship is *not* to be based on our own imagination and creativity.[6] "The law," said Calvin, "is a bridle to prevent men from turning aside to spurious worship," and, "Piety … confines itself within due bounds."[7] That is, true worship of God abides by the standards of God himself. The standard of Scripture trumps pragmatic concerns. Calvin is very strong on this point: "Nothing is more wicked than to contrive various modes of worship without the authority of the Word of God."[8] We should examine every part of our worship service in light of the

Bible. Calvin warned against "attempting anything in religion at random"[9] or based on good intentions.

A current trend is to allow contemporary culture rather than Scripture to determine the manner of the church's worship. Ironically, God specifically warns *against* this. Israel was not to follow the worship patterns of its unbelieving neighbors (Deuteronomy 12:29–32). God rather, exhorts his people to be careful to observe his commands, neither adding to nor taking away from them (Leviticus 10:1–3). The elders of the church, in particular, are given a solemn charge to guard the sacredness and scripturalness of the worship of God.

Not only is worship regulated by God's Word, it is also expressed through the Word. As W. Robert Godfrey has written,

> The churches of the Reformation (and to a significant extent also the churches before the Reformation) not only sought to have the Bible guide their worship, but also sought to fill worship with the Word of God. This is because the Word not only instructs us but is also the means through which we draw near to God. We know, serve, and worship God through his Word."[10]

Our worship services must breathe a spirit of Bible. The Word must saturate our services as we sing it, pray it, preach it, and receive it via the sacraments. If a stranger were to walk into your service at any point would he soon realize that your worship is an expression of the Word of God? As Godfrey asked, in relation to reading not just a verse or two of the Bible in public worship but large sections, "Do we really love the Word of God if we are content consistently to hear only a verse or two?"[11]

Heart Matters

As important as Scripture-regulated worship is, it's not enough. Worship must also be "in Spirit." In commenting on John 4:23,

Calvin said, "The worship of God is said to consist *in the Spirit*, because it is nothing else than that inward faith of the heart which produces prayer, and, next, purity of conscience and self-denial, that we may be dedicated to obedience to God as holy sacrifices."[12] There are at least four heart attitudes that God is searching for in true worshipers.

First, God is looking for sincerity. One of the regular charges Jesus levels at the Pharisees is that of hypocrisy (e.g. Mark 7:6). Hypocrisy is the lip service of a disinterested heart. A hypocrite is a pretender, literally one who wears a mask; in this case a mask of piety to cover his lack of true piety. There is a great danger in the show of religiosity in that we can hide from men the real situation of our hearts by lip service. Calvin said, "Nothing pleases [God] that is not accompanied by the inward sincerity of heart."[13] Hypocritical worship is cured by taking off the mask through confession. To confess means to tell God what he already knows about us: "unto whom all hearts be open, all desires known, and from whom no secrets are hid."[14] God isn't tricked by our masks.

Second, God is looking for humility. As we come before God with sincerity, another requisite attitude will be humility. True worship requires a brokenness of spirit: "The sacrifices of God are a broken spirit; a broken and contrite heart, O God, you will not despise" (Psalm 51:17). Our fallen-ness contrasts with God's glory: "For thus says the One who is high and lifted up, who inhabits eternity, whose name is Holy: 'I dwell in the high and holy place, and also with him who is of a contrite and lowly spirit'" (Isaiah 57:15). This is why one particularly fitting call to worship is: "Come let us worship and *bow down*" (Psalm 95:6).

Third, God is looking for joy. A true understanding of joy is not incompatible with but actually compliments humility. When we truly understand our humble circumstances in relation to the righteous God we are filled with inexpressible joy that he has condescended to fellowship with us in Christ. In this vein we are actually commanded to worship joyfully with singing (Psalm 95:1–2).

Fourth, God is looking for gratitude. Gratitude is the understanding that everything we have comes from God. As we mature in our faith we will be able to worship with thanks even in the midst of dire circumstances (Psalm 100:4; Acts 16:25).

At the conclusion of his book on predestination, R. C. Sproul explains the relationship between our election and worship. He says predestination

> is a theology that begins and ends with grace. It begins and ends with doxology. We praise a God who lifted us from spiritual deadness and makes us walk in high places ... It makes our souls rejoice to know that all things are working together for our good. We delight in our Savior who truly saves us and preserves us and intercedes for us ... We ponder mysteries and bow before them, but not without doxology for the riches of grace he has revealed.[15]

God's amazing grace, therefore, is ultimately what ties together the basis for our worship, the object of our worship, and the means of our worship.

Questions

If someone were to ask you why go to church, what could you say? In other words, why do we worship?

Offer some reflections on "seeker-sensitive" worship in light of John 4:23.Why is it critical to understand that Scripture regulates worship?

Why is it critical to understand that in worship, the attitude of the heart matters?

In what ways are we tempted to hypocritical worship?

For Further Reading

William Boekestein, "How to Grow Spiritually." (http://www. ligonier.org/blog/how-grow-spiritually/)

W. Robert Godfrey, *Pleasing God in Our Worship*, Today's Issues (Wheaton: Crossway Books, 1999).

Terry L. Johnson, *Reformed Worship: Worship that is According to Scripture* (Jackson, MS: Reformed Academic Press, 2000).

What is Reformed Worship, How to Plant a Reformed Church: The Church Planting Manual of the URCNA, https://www.urcna. org/urcna/Missions/ChurchPlantingManual/How%20to%20 Plant%20a%20Reformed%20Church.pdf (Accessed September 1, 2014).

Chapter Eight

The Practice of Our Worship

I was so overwhelmed with awe and joy. I had just come out from my first Reformed worship service. I kept thinking to myself, "Why didn't I find this earlier?" For the first time I felt that I didn't "go to church" but that I went to worship. The service was saturated in Scripture and filled with the assurance of the gospel from the call to worship to the absolution to the sermon to the Lord's Supper to the benediction. I had finally found what I was looking for.

In the previous chapter we sketched some essentials regarding worship: its basis being our calling and redemption, its object being the Triune God, and its means being the "spirit" of believing hearts and the "truth" of the Scriptures. This foundation of worship is extremely helpful but it still doesn't paint a comprehensive picture in terms of what a worshiping church will actually look like. But this picture begins to emerge when we implement biblical principles and imitate biblical and church-historical examples of worship.

What is a Worship Service?

A worship service is a corporate meeting with God that evokes from the worshiper a heart-felt declaration of the majesty and sufficiency of God. In the Bible it is evident that worship happens in the context of God meeting with redeemed man (Exodus 3:5, Isaiah 6:1–7, Hebrews 12:18–29, Revelation 4–5). When redeemed men and women in the Bible meet with God their response is one of "reverence and awe" (Hebrews 12:28).

There are several implications of this basic definition of a worship service. The first is that *worship is participatory.* This means that we don't come to worship to observe passively. We come to join our hearts actively in prayer and to add voices to the singing and recitation of liturgy. Unless you have had the privilege of leading worship, you may not realize how many attendees are apparently not participating.

Contrary to much contemporary worship, this principle of participatory worship applies to believers *and their children.* For hundreds of generations the worshipers of God have joined together as a whole body. The practice of removing children from the worship service is a relatively new invention reflective of our consumer-driven culture with its desire for choice and specialization. How many ushers tap unsuspecting moms on their shoulders to say, "I can show you where to take your child." What they mean is that the ordinary sounds a two-year old makes didn't fit in with the highly choreographed worship many churches have crafted. As the disciples rebuked those who brought little children to Jesus, Jesus rebuked them (Mark 10:13).[1]

The few glimpses that we have into New Testament worship services give clear indication that they were family events (Acts 10:33; 16:32). God's expectation that children should be present with adults during the Passover, one of the most sacred events in the Jewish calendar, is weighty evidence in favor of family-integrated services (Exodus 12:26–27). If nothing else, children who are present for corporate worship will be prompted to ask questions.

The second implication of worship as a corporate meeting with God is that *our response should be characterized by reverence and awe.* This is not to say that our approach to worship must be grave or severe. It *is* to say that our approach to worship should *not* be casual or frivolous since we are to "rejoice with trembling" (Psalm 2:12). The book of Hebrews compares and contrasts worship in the Old Testament age to that in the new. At Mount Sinai God's voice blasted like a trumpet and shook the earth (Hebrews 12:18–19, 25). The writer contrasts that experience with ours when he says, "You have not come to what may be touched ... but you have come to Mount Zion" (Hebrews 12:18, 22). He then goes on to say, "For if [those at Sinai] did not escape when they refused him who warned them on earth, much less will we escape if we reject him who warns from heaven. At that time his voice shook the earth, but now he has promised, 'Yet once more I will shake not only the earth but also the heavens'" (Hebrews 12:25–26). The point is that our God is by no means *less* of a consuming fire today than he was in the days of Moses (Hebrews 12:29). Our approach to worship should reflect the majesty and the glory of God.

Is There a "Shape" to Worship?
The notion of shape seems rather subjective to us. Is there a proper shape to a house, a shrub, or a person? Things come in all shapes and sizes, right? To some extent, this is true of worship. God hasn't revealed a blueprint that explains the precise shape New Testament worship should take. But this doesn't mean that a worship leader can "design" a worship service to take any shape he can conceive. God has revealed to us that shape, or form, matters. The essence of worship creates the form and shape of worship.

Order of Worship (Liturgy)
In the Old Testament God was *very* particular about the specifics of worship. He dictated with precision the "who, what, where, when and how" of worship. He also spelled out strict sanctions for violating his order. In the New Testament, with the church

coming to maturity (Galatians 3:19–4:7) a greater degree of freedom is given to God's children (Galatians 5:1). Nonetheless, God's insistence on order remains constant. For this reason he said, "all things should be done decently and in order" (1 Corinthians 14:40). This command comes in the context of Paul's teaching on church worship services.

The history of the church, likewise, calls us to an orderly worship. The orderly pattern of early Christian worship is revealed in such writings as *The Didache* (120 AD), Justin Martyr's *First Apology* (155 AD) and Tertullian's *Apology* (197 AD). In more recent history, the Reformers laid out biblically thoughtful orders of worship that modern worship leaders would do well to consult.[2] Some of the items in this liturgy are clear biblical requirements: the reading and preaching of the Word, the sacraments, and prayer (Acts 2:42). Others follow from biblical principle and example. It is our conviction that all are glorifying to God and edifying to the worshiper.

Dialogue

If God's Word and early Christian testimony give us examples of some of the elements in which our worship should consist, the question still remains, "How shall these elements be arranged?" Should we sing most of our songs in a cluster or should they be spread throughout the service? Where should the offering be plugged into the service (if, indeed it should be)? How should the service begin? How should it end?

Many of these questions are answered if we conceive of this corporate meeting with God as a dialogue or conversation. God has revealed himself in his Word as a communicator who graciously engages his people. In this conversation we see the steady pattern of God initiating and his people responding. God thundered to Job "out of the whirlwind and said, 'Dress for action like a man; I will question you, and you will make it known to me'" (Job 40:6–7). Job responded to God's Word by abhorring himself and repenting in dust and ashes (Job 42:6). In this example we learn that part of the dialogue of a worship service will be a Law/Repentance exchange; God speaks his law, revealing his holiness and we humble ourselves and repent of our sins. The same pattern emerges in Exodus 24 and Isaiah 6. Or, take Jesus' beautiful invitation recorded in John 7: "If anyone thirsts, let him come to me and drink. Whoever believes in me, as the Scripture has said, 'Out of his heart will flow rivers of living water'" (John 7:37–38). The Lord communicates the sufficiency of Christ and the merits of his righteousness and then calls us, in response, to believe. This same dialogical principle is evident in the Eucharistic element of a worship service. God confirms the unchangeable promise of his favor through the bread and wine. His people answer by coming to the Heavenly Table and receiving his gift for their souls.

What About the Particulars of Worship?

Worship is a corporate dialogue with the living God, which is governed by the Scripture (in truth) and evokes a response of believing reverence and gratitude (in spirit). This being the case, there are several elements that should, or at least could, compose a service of worship. Recognizing that many good orders of these elements might exist, we have organized them under two headings: God's speech and ours.

God Speaks to Us

When we consider that in the worship service God is speaking to us we need to be careful, first of all, not to become distracted by the man in the pulpit. The faithful minister is God's voice. He is merely an instrument. Still, God's pattern throughout history is to speak through human mediators (Hebrews 1:1–2). Below are several elements of worship in which God speaks to his people.

Call to Worship. The Psalms include many great texts, which can be used to alert God's gathered people that the worship service is beginning. Psalm 34:3 is one example: "Oh, magnify the Lord with me, and let us exalt his name together." God's call to worship is both a gracious invitation and an imperial summons. On a practical note, this is the time to put distractions behind you if you haven't already done so in silence before the service.

God's Greeting. The writer to the Hebrews reminds us that "our God is a consuming fire" (Hebrews 12:29). He has compared and contrasted New Testament and Old Testament worship in the previous verses. In both there is an element of fear (Isaiah 6). In the face of this fear we need confirmation that God is for us. "The Salutation is the greeting by which Christ reminds us that he is in our midst, bringing grace, mercy, and peace."[3] The greeting is like the golden scepter that King Ahasuerus extended toward Esther, indicating that she would not die for coming into his presence (Esther 8:4). And we enter the *heavenly* presence of the King of the universe.

Reading of the Law. This reminds us of God's holiness and convicts us of our sin and need for Christ. The law confirms that we cannot make things right by simply doing well. The law is also used to direct our paths in ways that are pleasing to God (HC, Q&A 115).

Assurance of Pardon. This point is sometimes called a declaration of forgiveness or absolution. The law reminds us of our sin in order that we might be revived by the gospel. Christ has given his ministers the authority to declare to the contrite and penitent that God forgives them for the sake of Christ (Matthew 18:18; John 20:23).[4]

Scripture Reading. Paul directed Timothy to give attention not only to exhortation and doctrine of Scripture but also to its reading (1 Timothy 4:13). Given how little Scripture is read even in Christian homes today, every Lord's Day our worship should feature sizeable portions of Scripture readings, preferably from both Testaments.

Sermon. The sermon is the exposition and application of Scripture focusing on provision of grace in Christ to fallen, believing sinners. It is not enough to just read Scripture; we need to understand it. The Ethiopian eunuch could not understand what he read until Philip explained it to him. God reproduces Philip's ministry through the preaching of his Word (Acts 8:26–40). The sermon is God's living Word to us (1 Thessalonians 2:13). As the Second Helvetic Confession says, "Wherefore when this Word of God is now preached in the church by preachers lawfully called, we believe that the very Word of God is preached, and received of the faithful" (Ch. 1).[5]

Benediction. The benediction is literally, God's "good word" pronounced at the conclusion of the worship service. In the worship of the Old Testament tabernacle and temple, Israel appeared before the face of the LORD . And one of the duties of the priests as they came out of this presence of God and before the people was to pronounce the blessing of the Lord upon them: "The LORD bless you and keep you; the LORD make his face to shine upon you and be gracious to you; the LORD lift up his countenance upon you and give you peace" (Numbers 6:24–26). In a similar way, the apostles' letters to the people of God ended with such benedictions: "The grace of the Lord Jesus Christ and the love of God and the fellowship of the Holy Spirit be with you all" (2 Corinthians 13:14). The benediction is a promise that God will actively abide with us by his Word and Spirit. The benediction sends forth the worshipers with an indelible impression of living before the face of God. In this, the benediction sums up the whole "liturgy." If the entire worship service were simply a reflection on the grace of the Lord Jesus Christ, the love of God the Father, and the fellowship of the Holy Spirit, it would still capture the heart of worship.

We Speak to God

Silent Prayer. Our lives are often a buzz of activity from the moment we wake up until our heads hit the pillow at night. For this reason we should take a few moments to prepare our hearts for worship prior to hearing God's call.

Invocation.[6] Historically this was known as the *votum*, which is a vow made by the people of God, often through the minister, in the words, "Our help is in the name of the Lord, who made heaven and earth" (Psalm 124:8; Cf. Psalm 79:13). It is a pledge of our own neediness and our dependence upon the God in whom we trust.

Confession of Sin. Believers confess their sins individually throughout the week on an ongoing basis. But corporate worship is a special time in which we confess our sins as a body of sinners. We do this through congregational prayer, through song, and through silent prayer throughout the service.

Singing. One of the most significant ways in which we speak to God during the worship service is through congregational song. Sadly, congregational singing has fallen on hard times. In a recent article entitled, "The Slow Death of Congregational Singing" one author suggests that, "Genuine, heartfelt congregational singing is experiencing its dying gasps."[7] This may be a bit melodramatic but it does draw our attention to a significant problem: robust congregational singing seems to be on the decline. There are several factors that may be contributing to this problem. It has been suggested that the excessive amplification of trained worship teams may actually discourage participation from the people in the pew. There is also the fact that many people in the church simply have never been trained how to sing so they don't feel comfortable doing it. Both of these factors could be addressed simply by providing musical training in the church and returning to an emphasis on the human tongue as the primary instrument in worship. Another hindrance to robust congregational singing is a pervasive fear of man and an atrophied view of God. When the smiles and frowns of man are weightier to us than the smiles and frowns of God then we will not offer to God the kind of worship through singing of which he is worthy. Moses offers a great insight to congregational singing when he said, "The Lord is my strength and my song, and he has become my salvation" (Exodus 15:2). When God becomes our ultimate expression, the way we approach congregational singing will be dramatically changed.

Confession of Faith. Believers in worship are not only to confess their sins but they are also to confess their faith. For centuries, Christians have expressed their faith through the words of the Apostles' and Nicene Creeds. These creeds not only focuses on the being and works of our Triune God, they also express the trust and confidence we have in this God. If the church is called to be a confessing community, it makes sense for us to first confess our faith before our brothers and sisters (Psalm 22:22, 25).

Prayer. There are several ways in which believers call upon God in prayer during worship. First, consider the congregational or pastoral prayer. You may ask, "What am *I* to do during the time the *pastor* prays?" Pray! Here are some suggestions to help congregants become more involved in the congregational prayer.

- Share prayer requests beforehand or have a list in the bulletin.

- Attentively follow the words of the minister.

- "Amen" the prayer privately throughout and have a corporate "Amen" at the conclusion.

- Incorporate congregational prayers into personal and family prayers.

Second, there is the prayer for illumination. Apart from God's illumination, the Bible will remain to us a closed book. We express our humility by seeking the Lord's help before we study his Word:

> Blessed Lord, who hast caused all holy Scriptures to be written for our learning; Grant that we may in such wise hear them, read, mark, learn, and inwardly digest them, that by patience and comfort of thy holy Word, we may embrace, and ever hold fast, the blessed hope of everlasting life, which thou has given us in our Savior Jesus Christ.[8]

Third, there is a prayer for application. The applicatory prayer after the sermon actually *is* application. When we ask God to work in us what he has taught us we are becoming "not hearers only" but doers of the Word (James 1:22).

Offering. While there is minor debate within modern Reformed churches over whether offerings belong in public worship, with some advocating an offering box outside the place of worship, we are assuming it does belong in public worship because of Paul's instructions, for example (1 Corinthians 16:2). As far as where it belongs in a service, it could be argued that one of the best places for the offering in the worship service is after the preaching of the gospel. In this way, Christian giving is what it should be, an expression of gratitude.

Christian worship is a corporate meeting with the God of heaven and earth. As such the way in which we approach him is of utmost importance. Our hope is that the preceding has at least helped spur you on to thoughtfully consider what the Bible says about how to worship God in spirit and truth.

Questions

What is a worship service?

What does the Bible say about the "shape" of a worship service?

What does "worship as dialogue" suggest about your involvement in worship?

In what ways can we participate when God speaks to us in worship?

How might Job 40:6–7 speak to a seeker-centered approach to worship?

Can you think of some ways of helping children to participate in worship?

For Further Reading

D. G. Hart and John R. Muether, *With Reverence and Awe: Returning to the Basics of Reformed Worship* (Phillipsburg, NJ: P&R Publishing, 2002).

Daniel R. Hyde, *What to Expect in Reformed Worship* (Eugene, OR: Wipf & Stock, second edition 2013).

R. C. Sproul, *Everyone's a Theologian: An Introduction to Systematic Theology* (Sanford, FL: Reformation Trust Publishing, 2014), 274–278.

Chapter Nine

A Witnessing Church

Several years ago the popular anti-Calvinist writer, Dave Hunt, summarized many evangelical Christians' opinions when he said that Calvinists "bring the gospel to the world not *because* of their Calvinism, but only *in spite* of it."[1] I remember hearing similar sentiments while in college, as I was first learning about the Reformation. The argument goes that since Reformed theology teaches eternal and unconditional election, therefore, no-matter-what the chosen are the chosen; since Reformed theology teaches Christ's satisfaction of God's justice on the cross is only effective for some, therefore, he cannot be offered to the world; since Reformed theology teaches all humanity is so dead in sin, therefore, it's pointless sharing the gospel with those who cannot even believe. Because of this, Calvinists can only inconsistently desire to bring the gospel to the world (a patently false assertion!).

As we will see below, though, a well-ordered and vibrant church does not exist merely for itself. We exist primarily for the glory of God. Secondarily, we exist for the edification of those inside the church *and* for the sake of the salvation of those outside in the world. The church is the light of the world (Matthew 5:14) and each congregation is to be a lampstand among which Jesus walks (Revelation 1:12). Because of who we are we are to be a witnessing church, engaging in the "ministry of reconciliation" (2 Corinthians 5:18). How can we as a local church put this mandate into practice?[2]

Thankfully, God has both explained and exemplified, demanded and demonstrated, his missionary mandate in both the Old and New Testaments. One of the best places to get a sense of God's missionary enterprise is to read the Book of Acts. Here we can observe the *practice* of a witnessing church. Seeing the outward-oriented church in action is a great encouragement to us. But it is also important to step back and consider some basic *principles* of missions. In this chapter we will consider five aspects of congregational witness and then in chapter 10 will consider the "how" of witnessing.

A Definition of Missions (What)

Christian mission is the church's grateful activity in response to the mission of the Triune God of grace (*Missio Dei*) who is actively calling the world to repentance and reconciliation with Himself.[3] Because God has entered into our world in the incarnation, death, and resurrection of Jesus Christ, the church goes out to that world.

And the church goes out with the ministry of reconciliation through gospel proclamation. Viewing missions as a ministry of reconciliation (2 Corinthians 5:18–21) helps us to view missions as the articulation of the great problem that exists between God and man as well as the plan to heal the breach. The outline of the book of Romans as well as of the Heidelberg Catechism (HC, Q&A 2) gives us a very practical summary of this ministry: sin (Romans 1:18–3:20), salvation (Romans 3:21–11:36), and service (Romans 12:1–16:27). Because "all have sinned and fall short of the glory of God" (Romans 3:23), we need a righteousness that comes from God himself (Romans 3:19–22). Because God freely gives this righteousness to his children, we are obliged to live lives of loving gratitude (Romans 12:1). This three-part outline helps us understand the importance of confronting unbelievers with the reality of their sin. After all, there is no need for a ministry of reconciliation if no problem exists between men and God for which humans need to repent. But given this problem, the promise of the gospel shines more brightly: whoever believes in Christ crucified shall not perish but have eternal life. Finally, those who have been grafted into the body of Christ, the church, are equipped to live as reconciled children of God. In other words, the work of reconciliation consists of estranged people joining the holy body of Jesus.

Some will consider this definition of missions to be overly narrow. Doesn't this definition exclude lots of things that we typically consider to be "missions?" What about "short-term missions," those who work on missions fields, as well as everyday issues such as friendship, hospitality, diaconal work, a hearty work ethic, and social justice? In fact, there are many more things that can assist missions by preparing or following up on the preached Word but the mission that King Jesus left to his church is that of reconciling lost sinners through gospel-centered disciple making (Matthew 28:18–20). Missionary activity, properly speaking is the announcement of the gospel of Jesus Christ. Still, there should be a close relationship between Word and deed ministry; the two should go together with Word ministry taking priority. Such an ordering of a Word and deed ministry seems rather counter cultural today. We hear churches with slogans like, "Just do good," taking the line supposed uttered by St. Francis of Assissi, "Preach the Gospel at all times and when necessary use words." As popular as this approach seems to be today, it is simply not the pattern we see in the New Testament. The deeds of the church gave credibility to her words.

What we see, instead, is the centrality of preaching in missions. Scripture spells this out when it says, "faith comes from hearing, and hearing through the word of Christ" (Romans 10:17). Preaching repentance and faith, whether in an established local church, or beyond its scope is mission activity.

Still, the question remains, "What shall the ambassadors of Christ communicate?" The answer given by regular apostolic pattern is this: proclaim the completed work of Christ as well as the sinner's need to believingly respond. This means that the gospel is about what God has done through Christ. He satisfies the justice of God in his substitutionary death. As the Canons of Dort say, "The promise of the gospel is that whosoever believes in Christ crucified shall not perish, but have eternal life" (CD 2.5).[4] Clearly, this promise requires a response on the part of the sinner. We must present Christ himself in his suffering, his death, resurrection, conquest and glory and say, "What will you do with him?" (John 19:14). This presentation of Christ is both a gracious invitation and a powerful command. You *must* be born again (John 3:7). Paul presented the Gospel message to the Athenians and then told them that God "now … commands all people everywhere to repent" (Acts 17:30).

Of course, the Christian ambassador does not simply proclaim the basic elements of the faith. Missionary activity is sometimes conceived of as stripping the message of God down to its "bare essentials." This may be a place to start but Jesus' Great Commission specifically mandates a comprehensive approach. Jesus specifically commands his missionaries to teach new disciples to live by every word that proceeds from the mouth of God (Deuteronomy 8:3; Matthew 28:20). This means that for us to understand and implement a biblical view of missions we must be convinced that missions rests on the centrality, sufficiency, efficiency, uniqueness, and authority of preaching.[5]

The Agent of Missions (Who)
Ultimately the Bible describes the agent of missions as the Triune

God himself, but he also works through the means of proclaimers of his Word. Let's take the latter first.

The Church Led by Its Officers

The church is the only institution in the world that has been divinely authorized to carry out the Great Commission (Matthew 16:18–19; 18:18; 28:19–20; Acts 1:8; 2 Corinthians 5:18–20). This does not mean that the implications of the Great Commission are limited to ordained ministers on behalf of organized churches. But the fact that Jesus' commission spoken to the apostles is rooted in preaching and baptizing, strongly suggests that the primary vehicle of Christian missions is the office of minister of the Word and Sacraments. This assertion does not detract from the sense in which all believers are to participate in the mission of God. It simply helps define roles. Believers have a responsibility in missions as "missionary helpers." Every believer can assist in the diaconal work through giving and volunteering in the various ministries the deacons oversee (Philippians 4:10–20) as well as through prayer (1 Thessalonians 5:25; 2 Thessalonians 3:1–2). We all should assist the ministry of the Word through encouragement, support, and receptiveness. Every believer is called to engage his peers by personally explaining the reason for his hope (see chapter 10). But none of this is to be done in isolation from the church of Jesus Christ.

The Bible's insistence on an ecclesiastical emphasis in missions also raises questions about para-church organizations. Is there a place for them? If the work of missions, properly speaking is a church function then it should be conducted under the authority of elders and through the support of deacons. Missionaries should not be accountable to a board or network but to the leaders of an organized church of Christ. Still, para-church organizations can be used of God to support the work of the church through specialized efforts which churches may not be able to provide themselves. For example, para-church groups play an important role in preparing missionaries for service through colleges, seminaries, and language institutes. The priority of the mission of the church over that of para-church organizations should also impact the way congregants and congregations tithe. Honest para-church organizations tell their audience that their first responsibility is to give to the local church.

God's Role in Missions

While it is proper to identify the church as the only divinely authorized missionary institution we need to remember that God himself is *the* missionary. All of the persons of the Trinity are active in missions. The Father gives "all authority" for missions to the Son (Matthew 28:18). The Son commissions the apostles to "go" (Matthew 28:18). The Spirit is sent by the Father and the Son to accomplish this missionary task (Acts 2). For this reason, the baptism of new converts is in the name of the Father, and the Son, and the Holy Spirit (Matthew 28:19). It is God who powerfully witnesses to himself through his word (Acts 14:3). He is the missionary, we are his instruments, his "jars of clay" (2 Corinthians 4:7). He saves all those who are appointed unto eternal life (Acts 13:48). This biblically God-centered view of missions helps mitigate disappointment in the mission field. After all, this is God's mission. We're just along for the ride.

The Time and Place of Missions (When, Where)

God has committed to us the task of reconciliation "to the end of the age" (Matthew 28:20). If we remember that the day of Christ's return is unknown to all men (Matthew 24:36; 1 Thessalonians 5:1–2) and that God will roll up the scroll of history in his own timing we will avoid the disappointments that often follow failed "evangelization-of-the-world-in-this-generation" plans, which are usually tied to an over, or under-realized eschatology. Of course, it is good to set goals; we should set *lofty* goals. But, a biblical plan for missions will avoid the corner cutting that often characterizes an imminent eschatology. The fact that God has not yet sent his

Son to judge the world indicates his graciousness as well as our duty to continue in the work (2 Peter 3:9). Jesus encourages us to continue when he says, "I am with you always, to the end of the age" (Matthew 28:20). Until then, we are to be "salt" and "light" (Matthew 5:13–16).

As mission work must be the prerogative of the church throughout the age, we must also carry this work out throughout the whole world. The promise of the gospel, "together with the command to repent and believe, ought to be declared and published to all nations, and to all persons promiscuously and without distinction, to whom God out of His good pleasure sends the gospel" (CD 2.5). Jesus gave the command: "Go into all the world and proclaim the gospel to the whole creation" (Mark 16:15). This text is a powerful reminder that the church has no right to exist in its own bubble. The church is not about us. Israel was to be a light to the nations (Isaiah 49:6). So is the church.

But the command to publish the gospel abroad equally requires that the ministry of reconciliation be alive and well in our own churches. The gospel is for believes and unbelievers *in the church*. In the words of the Heidelberg Catechism, the preaching of the gospel opens and shuts the kingdom of heaven when

> ... it is proclaimed and openly witnessed to believers, one and all, that as often as they accept with true faith the promise of the Gospel, all their sins are really forgiven them of God for the sake of Christ's merits; and on the contrary, to all unbelievers and hypocrites, that the wrath of God and eternal condemnation abide on them so long as they are not converted. According to this testimony of the Gospel, God will judge men both in this life and in that which is to come (HC, Q&A 84).[6]

The Reason for Missions (Why)
The final area of consideration has to do with motivation.

Why should the people of God be zealous for the ministry of reconciliation?[7] We should never have the attitude that "if God wants to save ____, he'll do it without us."

One reason is the promise of reward. At one point in their ministry, the apostles seem to question the worthiness of following Jesus. Peter speaks for them: "See, we have left our homes and followed you." Then we read Jesus' reply: "Truly, I say to you, there is no one who has left house or wife or brothers or parents or children, for the sake of the kingdom of God, who will not receive many times more in this time, and in the age to come eternal life" (Luke 18:28–30). The Scriptures seem to suggest that God's gracious blessings to us in heaven reflect our faithfulness here on earth (1 Corinthians 3:14–15; Matthew 25:14–30; Revelation 21:14). Certainly, a missionary mindset is part of that faithfulness.

Second, we should be motivated to the work of mission out of regard for the lost. At the end of the book of Jonah, God asks, "Should I not pity Nineveh, that great city, in which are more than 120,000 persons who do not know their right hand from their left?" (Jonah 4:11) God is contrasting Jonah's concern for the temporal (the plant that grew up overnight) with his lack of concern for the eternal (the never-dying souls of men). The fact that the text leaves the question unanswered calls us to reflect on our own answer.[8] This concern led those who embraced Reformed theology to be pioneers in modern missions. The Reformed church of Geneva sent missionaries to Brazil in the 1550s. John Eliot (1604–1690) went every other week to preach to and catechize the children of native Americans in Massachusetts beginning in 1646. The Church of England created the "Society for the Propagation of the Gospel in New England" in the seventeenth century. The Synod of Dort began a missionary school. David and John Brainerd preached to the Housatonic people in the mid-1700s. William Carey, the "father of modern missions," founded what came to be called the London Missionary Society. Robert Moffat (1795–1883) and David

Livingstone (1813–1873) gave themselves to South and Central Africa. Robert Morrison (1782–1834) translated the Bible into Chinese by 1818. And the list goes on!

A third reason to be actively engaged in missions is the well being (*bene esse*) of the church. A non-witnessing church will not be healthy. Not only will the non-witnessing church stagnate as a result of self-centered disobedience but also because God's design for the sanctification, maturity and growth of the church includes a regular influx of new, "rough-edged" worshipers. Jesus warns this kind of non-witnessing church, saying to it "I have *this* against you, that you have left your first love." (Revelation 2:4; NASB). It could be argued on the basis of the Great Commission (Matthew 28:18–20), that a church that fails to reflect the apostolic example of going out with a mission to the world is in danger of losing its right to the name "church" (Cf. Revelation 2:5).

Fourth, congregational witnessing is a must if we are concerned about the good of our community, country, and world. With all the bad news in society, it is easy to think that the only thing left to do is complain about it. But if we really believe that Jesus is the answer to the poverty, crime, and ugliness in our cities and world we stop talking about our problems and start talking about Jesus!

A fifth motivation for congregational witness is the command of God. The Great Commission is not the "Good Suggestion." In no uncertain terms Jesus declares, "You will be my witnesses!" (Acts 1:8).

But the most significant reason why the church must be a witnessing church is the glory of God. When the gospel is proclaimed, God is glorified. He is glorified when sinners repent upon hearing that message. He is glorified when his people speak his name (Psalm 34:4). John Piper has famously said,

Missions is not the ultimate goal of the church. Worship is. Missions exists because worship doesn't. Worship is ultimate not missions, because God is ultimate, not man .... Worship, therefore, is the fuel and goal of missions. It's the goal of missions because in missions we simply aim to bring the nations into the white-hot enjoyment of God's glory. The goal of missions is the gladness of the people in the greatness of God.[9]

With so many weighty reasons to witness to the justice and mercy of God, our final question regarding congregational witnessing should be asked with a tone of eager anticipation: "How?" We hope to give some practical answers to this question in the next chapter.

Questions

Why is it important to understand the gospel message, and gospel ministry, in terms of reconciliation?

Why are words, and not deeds alone, essential for true witness?

What are some of the dangers of "missionary activity" detached from a local church?

Elaborate on why a non-witnessing church will not be healthy.

Explain the correlation between worship and witness.

How will church officers lead the way in witnessing in a well-ordered church?

For Further Reading

J. H. Bavinck, *An Introduction to the Science of Missions* (Philadelphia: The Presbyterian and Reformed Publishing Co., 1960).

C. John Miller, *Outgrowing the Ingrown Church* (Grand Rapids: Zondervan 1986).

John R. W. Stott, *Christian Mission in the Modern World: What the Church Should be Doing Now!* (Downers Grove, IL: InterVarsity Press, 1975).

Chapter Ten

The Practice of a Witnessing Church

I can remember the feelings I had about evangelism and missions in the first couple of years after I was converted to Christ. If I wasn't witnessing to my unbelieving family every day and inviting them to church every week I felt like such a failure. And when short-term missions trips were announced in church, since I didn't have the money to go, I felt like such a second-tier Christian. Fast-forward several years to my becoming a pastor, and I have found a disturbing trend. It seems that so many Christians who were in evangelical churches like I was but who then become members in a Reformed church feel so relieved by the gospel's freedom from unbiblical legalism, that they seem to forget about the lost.

Unfortunately, for many churches and Christians, evangelism and missions is an appendix rather than a core component of their task. Such churches tend to be precautious rather than prevailing, busy preserving the faith within, not propagating it with out. Precautious churches know little about taking risks and a lot about minimal survival.[1] They exist largely to meet the needs of church members. For them community means the church is a subculture that is closed to outsiders. Lost people are neither pursued evangelistically nor welcomed enthusiastically. Non-witnessing churches are definitely not well-ordered.

A well-ordered church is a witnessing church. As we learned in the last chapter, the Great Commission was given to the officers of the church who were to fulfill it by means of preaching and administering the sacraments. In saying this one could quickly and falsely assume that missions and evangelism is an endeavor of the officers of the church only. But such an assumption fails to see the church as both an *organization* and as an *organism*. This dual identity of the church is critical for a proper understanding of missions.

The church as organization refers to its formal structure. The organizational church functions through the offices and means that God has instituted. Formal missionary activity should be the work of the organized church through the preaching of the Word, the administration of the sacraments, and discipline.

But the church doesn't exist simply because of its formal structure of leadership; it is also a living body. The congregation's life as an organism pulses through the living membership of believers. Herein lies the concern with evangelism committees where energies can be spent more in administration than action. Organization is important but "we must be careful not to remove the work from its grass roots through administrative machinery to boards, or other centralized agencies."[2] All Christians share in Christ's anointing with the Holy Spirit (HC, Q&A 32). We are prophets, confessing the name of Christ (Matthew 10:32). We are part of a royal priesthood (1 Peter 2:9), called to intercessory prayer on behalf of lost souls. We are kings who strive for the extension of his kingdom through spiritual means (Revelation 1:6).

How does the church, as both an institution and an organism strive to fulfill the Great Commission? To answer this question in an organized and practical way, we have divided the missional task of the church into three parts: *foreign* witnessing, *congregational* witnessing, and *personal* witnessing. Each of these parts says something about how the church functions as an organization (or institution) and how it functions as an organism (or individuals).

"Foreign" Witnessing

Foreign witnessing refers to missionary outreach conducted beyond of the scope of the local church's native land. This type of witnessing reflects Paul's aim, "to preach the gospel, not where Christ has already been named" (Romans 15:20). This foreign mission field takes place in the "ends of the world" where the church has little to no presence.

It is our belief that foreign field witnessing should be undertaken in connection with a properly organized church through the preaching of the Word, administration of sacraments, and administration of discipline under the oversight of elders. A central goal of missionary activity is to reconcile sinners to the Lord, making them a part of the body of Christ. Because the church as organization is the culmination of the gathering of the church as organism, the goal of foreign field witness is to organize local churches as God is pleased to draw people to himself in a particular region. Christ's Great Commission is not merely to make converts but to build churches. This means that a primary form of missionary outreach is church planting and is, arguably, "the most effective evangelistic methodology known under heaven."[3]

Foreign field witnessing as church planting is consistent with the emphasis of churches in Acts. On his missionary journeys, Paul planted the seeds of the gospel in virgin soil. By God's grace, a few years later, he was able to write epistles to the various churches he had been instrumental in founding. To say it differently, Paul wasn't just preaching the gospel; he was planting churches. He and the other missionaries in Acts organized churches by appointing elders

(Acts 14:23). Paul maintained regular contact with the fledgling churches through personal visitation and letter writing (Acts 15:41).

Church planting in foreign fields seems somewhat "distant" from the local churches to which you and I belong. But there are at least three important ways local congregations can be involved in foreign field witnessing.

Financial Involvement

Paul makes plain that Christian churches have an obligation to financially support the men whom God has called to the ministry of the word (2 Corinthians 11:8–9; 1 Timothy 5:17–18). One indicator of the church's commitment to the Great Commission is the extent to which church planters are being funded. It is amazing how many "good causes" our churches are supporting while our church planters spend so much of their time fundraising. There are a million and one causes that your local church could be supporting; but our priority should be to fund ordained ministers planting churches. This means that our congregations need to be allocating a sizeable portion of our spending to foreign missions.

Relational Involvement

It is customary for a missionary to be sent out to his field by a "laying-on-of-hands" ceremony (Acts 13:3). One of the reasons that representatives of a congregation lay their hands on missionaries prior to their departure is to indicate their commitment to and solidarity with them.[4] In the laying on of hands, the congregation is saying to those being sent out: "We love you, we support you, our hearts are with you." The implication is, that long after the laying on of hands ceremony is over, those sending and those being sent will maintain a relational involvement in the mission.

Christians in the sending church have a responsibility to maintain some level of contact with those whom they are supporting. We should be diligent to read the updates they send.

We should write to our missionaries. Some churches assign to each of their members a foreign missionary, urging them to maintain regular written contact with that missionary (without it becoming a burden to them). When possible, the local church should send a delegation to visit the mission field. As expensive as this is, it can be extremely valuable. There is no better way to encourage those in the sending church than by first hand peer accounts of the work.

Prayerful Involvement

Finally, believers must maintain a relationship of prayer with their foreign field missionaries. Paul, himself asked for prayer from his supporting churches (1 Thessalonians 5:25; 2 Thessalonians 3:1; cf. Hebrews 13:18). We should pray for our missionaries as families and as a congregation. They are on the front lines of kingdom warfare. We pray for our country's soldiers but do we pray for the front line soldiers in God's kingdom?

Congregations that are financially, relationally, and prayerfully involved in foreign field witnessing will have thoughtful persons serving as liaisons between the congregation and the missionaries. One of the best ways to insure *little* interest in and giving toward any missionary endeavor is to fail to provide timely and pertinent information to the congregation regarding the mission. If the average person in your congregation cannot talk in meaningful and current terms about their missionaries, there is a problem.

Congregational Witnessing

Moving closer to home, local congregations must also be witnessing churches.[5] Not surprisingly, we are convinced that local congregational witnessing must be built around the preaching of the Word of God. Somehow, the preaching can get lost in the shuffle of a well-intentioned congregation's desire to be salt and light in their community. But we can't forget God's ordained means of effecting the reconciliation of fallen sinners is "hearing through the word of Christ" (Romans 10:17). This is why the Westminster

Larger Catechism speaks of the Word, sacraments, and prayer as the particular "outward and ordinary means whereby Christ communicates to his church the benefits of his mediation (WLC, Q&A 154).

Many Christian churches are committed to preaching the gospel of grace to anyone who will listen. We would love to see people come through our doors so they can hear carefully prepared, biblically inspired, earnestly delivered sermons. Picking up on Paul's string of questions in Romans 10, we must also ask, "How can we preach to them if they don't come to listen?" Most churches don't experience a steady stream of unreached people walking through their doors without a plan on the part of the church.[6]

There are usually three ways of describing how the church engages in missions. We'll exaggerate these ways for sake of clarity. *Attractional* churches put on huge programs to attract people to their church. They adopt the "Field of Dreams" mentality: if you build an impressive enough church with enough "relevant" programs, they will come. There are other churches which prefer instead to send their members out as personal missionaries; the *incarnational* model. In this model the witnessing doesn't happen in the church building but in backyards and coffee shops. The public ministry of the church is downplayed in favor of a more "organic" subtle approach. The third group, into which too many churches fall, is the *lackadaisical* model! Non-missional churches simply hope that visitors will show up to the church, perhaps because of a phone book ad. They assume that their members will witness for Christ by living generally decent lives. This latter category has either a skewed view of the sovereignty of God—God is so sovereign so I have no responsibilities—or they have lost their focus on the gospel all together. Assuming you agree that this third method is a non-method, we would propose a modified two-fold approach: an attractional approach and an incarnational approach. Churches should attempt to use biblical means to both draw in the lost (Isaiah 42:6) as well as to send out the redeemed (John 17:18). While the term "incarnational" is something of a trendy buzz word today, it is helpful. It is not meant to communicate that we somehow "make" Christ present in terms of his Incarnation, but that Christ is present in and through us in the world.

Attractional Model

If it weren't for the black eye given to the attractional model by some mega-churches, most Christians would readily recognize it as a scriptural model. The God-given symbolism of the church as light directs us to be visible, helpful and inviting (Isaiah 49:6; 60:3; Matthew 5:14–16). As the night watchman yearns for morning light (Psalm 130), so the church is called to be a winsome reflection of a gracious, calling God.

We see the attractional model functioning in the call to worship. Some of the calls to worship that populate the Psalms are plainly extended to the "unchurched." We are to declare God's glory among the nations (Psalm 96:3) that the nations would give him glory (Psalm 96:7). But how will they do so? They are called to come into the courts of the Lord to worship him (Psalm 96:9). The people of God are instruments of calling those outside the church to join them in the worship of the God of heaven and earth.

What are some practical suggestions for attracting people to the church? Be thoughtful about advertising through various media and other positive ways to promote the Word in your church.[7] To do this well, you might consider having a media coordinator in your church. If we believe we have something to offer to others then we should be bold in promoting it. Work on developing a positive reputation in the community through your people. As much as possible make your facility inviting to visitors. If your community could benefit from a clothing drive, organize one in your church building. Do you have people in your church that could help the underemployed secure jobs? Offer an employment seminar. Live in an immigrant community? Consider offering English as a Second Language courses at the church. The trend today seems to be to minimize the role of the organized church in witnessing. But God is still calling us to be light in his world.

Incarnational Model

If an attractional model is about getting people to the church, an incarnational model is about getting the church to the people, about meeting people in natural and meaningful ways.

Jesus is the ultimate justification for an incarnational model of outreach. He came to us because we could not and would not come to him. While on this earth Jesus traveled the countryside and preached to huge crowds that might not have listened to him had the venue been more formal. Paul, likewise, traveled from city to city, engaging people where he could. The prophet Jonah teaches us that God commands his servants to go to where the people who need to hear the message are. God was going to work a revival among the Ninevites. But he wasn't going to make them all travel to Israel to hear the call to repentance and faith!

How, can we meet unbelievers on their terms and turf? Begin by remembering the principle: face-to-face is best. We need to make opportunities for our churches to get out and meet people. If your situation has a civic celebration of some kind, take advantage by setting up a media table next to the beer tent and funnel cake wagon! You may find that you make more contacts with unbelievers in a day or more at a street fair than over the course of the entire year. You may also engage in neighborhood canvassing.[8] Our intention here, unlike that of the Jehovah's Witnesses, is not necessarily to challenge the beliefs of our neighbors but to attempt to engage them positively. Let them know you care about your community and that they are wanted at your church. You might leave resources, and hopefully a positive impression of the church.[9]

Although face-to-face may be best, we shouldn't neglect opportunities to distribute the preached Word through available media. Those who aren't coming to our church might be wiling to listen to messages on their own terms. Paul wrote letters and urged their circulation (Colossians 4:16). Many cities have a public access cable TV channel which will air local worship services, sometimes for free. Churches can leave audio CDs in restaurants and gas stations. Members can share sermons with their friends online.

Personal Witnessing

Many good books have been written on the topic of personal witnessing.[10] Rather than try to set forth a comprehensive plan for personal witnessing we will give attention to two of the most significant roadblocks to personal evangelism: lack of motivation and lack of method.

Lack of Motivation

It is a sad fact that many church members do not share the gospel because they don't know what it is or they don't believe it matters. There is no doubt that we struggle with unbelief. God knows this and he will forgive us when we repent of this sin and ask for forgiveness. But let's *struggle* with unbelief. We cannot give in to it and say, "I guess I'm never going to share the gospel." This may be an indication that we don't believe it ourselves. If you possessed the cure for cancer but didn't share it with anyone else we would have to conclude one of three things. Perhaps you are unaware that you possess such a cure. Perhaps you don't believe that it will actually work. Perhaps you don't care about those who are perishing of cancer. Do you believe the gospel? Do you believe that you were bound for hell without Jesus?

The classic text for personal witnessing assumes that those witnessing for Christ actually possess the hope they profess: "but in your hearts honor Christ the Lord as holy, always being prepared to make a defense to anyone who asks you for a reason for the hope that is in you; yet do it with gentleness and respect" (1 Peter 3:15). It's interesting that these two adjectives, "gentleness" (*prautēs*) and "respect" (*phobos*), seem to suggest that we witness gently to our neighbors while showing reverence to Christ the Lord.[11]

Lack of Method

Many of us don't witness because we lack a method. Here are some basic ideas. First, *begin close to home*. Many of us have rather small circles of regular contacts. But this doesn't mean that we have no opportunities to witness to the gospel. In other words, all Christians need to be taught and trained in friendship evangelism.

Second, *be intentional and proactive*. Engage in welcoming hospitality. View your home as a place of evangelism and witnessing, inviting unbelieving family and neighbors to hear and see the love of Christ for sinners. Invite your neighbors to worship.

Third, *utilize media*. Individual Christians have an incredible opportunity today to direct their friends to Christian media through social networking.[12] Share print and electronic sermons with neighbors. Don't forget about the nearly lost media form of letter writing. If you find difficulty speaking boldly about Christ in face-to-face conversations with an acquaintance or relative put it in writing.

Fourth, *maintain a good reputation*. Our witness is seriously hampered when our lives openly conflict with our faith. As Jesus taught, it was because of our "light," our good works, that unbelievers would come to glorify God (Matthew 5:14–16).

We want to be sure to not end this chapter on a note of guilt. The work of salvation is the Lord's. It's his mission. If we believe that, and if we are convinced that he is graciously saving us from the guilt and power of sin, then let's remember to thank him and ask him for the courage to communicate these grand truths to others.

Questions

How can you be more relationally engaged in the foreign field witnessing of your church?

How familiar are you with the various causes and missionaries supported by your church? Are you *personally* giving to the work of foreign field missions?

Discuss the advantages, and possible disadvantages of the attractional model of congregational outreach.

Discuss the advantages, and possible disadvantages of the incarnational model of congregational outreach.

What challenges do you face in personal witnessing? How might these challenges be met with greater faithfulness?

For Further Reading

The Grand Rapids Board of Evangelism of the Christian Reformed Churches, *Reformed Evangelism: A Manual on Principles and Methods of Evangelization* (Grand Rapids: Baker Books House, 1948).

Roger S. Greenway, ed., *The Pastor-Evangelist: Preacher, Model, and Mobilizer for Church Growth* (Phillipsburg: Presbyterian and Reformed Publishing Company, 1987).

R. B. Kuiper, *God-Centered Evangelism: A Presentation of the Scriptural Theology of Evangelism* (Grand Rapids: Baker Book House, 1961), 111–171.

Will Metzger, *Tell the Truth: The Whole Gospel to the Whole Person by Whole People* (Downer's Grove, IL: Inter-Varsity Press, 1981).

Chapter Eleven

A Repenting Church

I t was my first vacation after being ordained to the ministry. We had been laboring for about a year, non-stop, without a break. It was time to recharge. Upon returning home my voicemail was full. The honeymoon was over and there was serious sin with a member of our core group. I came to realize that church discipline was the messy mark of a church as it was time to call a backslidden member to repentance.

The forgoing chapters have attempted to set a biblically-high standard for what the church is and what we as the church are called to do. The trouble with high standards, of course, is that they are hard to reach. Any church (or individual) that assumes it is completely meeting the standard of the Word is either ignorant of God's standards or blind to its own shortcomings—or both. It may be hard for us to admit but we fall far short of God's perfect pattern for the church. The good news is that God has an answer for the failures of the church's leaders and of its members. It's called repentance. In the Bible, repentance is first a change of mind (*metanoeō*; 2 Timothy 2:24–26) that leads to a change on the way of life (*epistrephō*; 1 Thessalonians 1:9). This happens once and for all at conversion—when we repent and believe.

But the church is also called to a constant life of repentance. Jesus pointedly tells five of the seven churches in Revelation to repent because they were heading in the wrong directions (Revelation 2:5; 2:16; 2:22; 3:3; 3:19). This message was not just for them, but for the church of Jesus Christ spanning the time from Christ's first coming to his second. Repentance is to be a regular, daily activity for believers in the church this side of glory. When we pray, "Forgive us our debts," a part of what we pray is for God to "pardon our daily failings" (WLC, Q&A 194). The problem is that we are naturally more likely to *approve* of our thoughts, words, and deeds rather than *repent* of them. So how can we be a repenting church?

God has given us a means of repentance called church discipline. Unfortunately, discipline is often thought of in purely *negative* and *vindicatory* terms. But according to Scripture, discipline is not merely the spiritual consequences of falling into sin and failing to repent of it, but first and foremost the *positive* and *loving* shepherding of the church's pastors, elders, and fellow members. Church discipline always has the goal and prayer of restored fellowship with God and man through repentance.

The Principles of Church Discipline
The principles of Christian church discipline can be expressed well in the following points.

Discipline is God's Loving Design
To properly appreciate the idea of church discipline we need to realize that it is a gift of a loving Father: "For the Lord disciplines the one he loves" (Hebrews 12:6). God compares the way that a loving parent disciplines a child to the way he disciplines believers (Hebrews 12:7–11). He takes pains to point out that discipline is painful but necessary and profitable. Through discipline God reveals his Fatherly love and care for us his children. God's design for discipline flows from his infinite and loving wisdom in our lives.

How often do parents discipline with mixed motives, faulty logic, and sinful passion? We're ashamed to answer. But God always disciplines his children for their good (Hebrews 12:10).

Discipline is Mandated by God

If we fail to grasp God's loving design for discipline, we might stumble over the instruments God uses to discipline his children. God does discipline his people toward maturity through natural and supernatural means. He can use financial crises, deteriorating health, or natural disasters to get our attention. He can also work directly on our hearts and consciences, convicting us of sin and giving us a yearning for holiness. By faith we can say that, "Whatever evil He sends upon me in this troubled life, He will turn to my good; for He is able to do it, being Almighty God, and willing also, being a faithful Father" (HC, Q&A 26).[1]

Christians are more likely to balk at God's chastening when it is administered by human means. Yet, God clearly commits to believers the duty of exhorting each other, "that none of you may be hardened by the deceitfulness of sin" (Hebrews 3:13). The classic text on church discipline, Matthew 18, consists of a series of imperatives or commands. Church discipline is not an option; it is an obligation. The churches of "Pergamus and Thyatira are reproved for harboring heretical teachers and heathen abominations" (Revelation 2:14; 2:20; 2:24) and bound to take disciplinary action.[2] In fact, when believers fail to exercise spiritual discipline, the church might expect to experience severe chastening from God's almighty hand (1 Corinthians 11:30–32).

Discipline is Good for God's Children

When God's children stray off the path and engage in destructive behaviors they need to be shaken by a sound rebuke (Titus 1:13). The man who has developed an unhealthy habit of not treating his wife with the equality that a sister in Christ and a partner in marriage deserves is to be confronted by his Christian brothers. If he is wise, the rebuke will do him good (Proverbs 9:8). The wife who speaks poorly of her husband behind his back, likewise needs to be reproved. If she has an obedient ear her rebuker will be to her "like a gold ring or an ornament of gold" (Proverbs 25:12). A fool refuses correction (Proverbs 15:12) because he doesn't realize it is for his good. A wise man welcomes reproof because he realizes that thereby he gets knowledge (Proverbs 21:11). As the wise preacher said, "Better was a poor and wise youth than an old and foolish king who no longer knew how to take advice" (Ecclesiastes 4:13).

Discipline is Good for God's Church
If discipline is good on the individual level it is critical on a congregational level. Paul explains that congregational sin is like a cancer that affects the whole body. It needs to be treated before the whole body is infected (1 Corinthians 5:5–6). A church will not be well-ordered if it allows sickness to flourish internally. Sometimes private confrontations are effective in rooting out the folly that can impact an entire congregation (Proverbs 13:20). Other times, when the sin is public or egregious, or the sinner recalcitrant, the rebuke cannot remain private. When sinners are rebuked publicly the rest of the congregation is given a reminder of the seriousness of sin (1 Timothy 5:20).

Discipline is Good for God's Glory
The church is a reflection of God. When rebellion is permitted in the church of God, his reputation suffers. In Ezekiel 20, God explains that he disciplined the rebellious generation in the desert "for the sake of my name, that it should not be profaned in the sight of the nations" (v. 14). A broken-down house can reflect poorly on its owner. The church is the household of God (Ephesians 2:19). When she tolerates disrepair she scorns her calling to be that mirror that reflects God's glory.

The Practice of Discipline

How should this principle above be put into practice? We offer the following three aspects of practical discipline.

Self-Discipline

The exercise of Christian discipline is first of all a personal duty of every child of God. As a coach is apt to say, "A chain is only as strong as its weakest link. Don't be that weak link!" Reform in the church needs to begin with each of us.

The practice of self-discipline begins with self-examination. David called upon God, "Search me, O God, and know my heart! Try me, and know my thoughts! And see if there be any grievous way in me, and lead me in the way everlasting" (Psalm 139:23–24). The implication of this request is that David also made a habit of testing himself. Believers are called to regularly examine themselves (1 Corinthians 11:28; 2 Corinthians 13) since the unexamined life can easily grow cold to God and his will. Paul gives a list of both the works of the flesh and the fruit of the Spirit as criteria for self-examination (Galatians 5:16–26). He says that both are plain to see if we will only examine ourselves (Galatians 5:19).

What does self-examination look like? First, it consists of humility and honesty before God and man. We confess the doctrine of total depravity but we fail to own how this doctrine affects us personally where the rubber hits the road. Second, we should examine ourselves with the help of a trusted spiritual friend. As we age we are encouraged to undergo regular physical checkups. What about regular *spiritual* checkups? Without the help of others we tend to make God's standards subjectively fit our proclivities. Third, we should take note of those whom God has given us for examples, the leaders of his church (Philippians 3:17). The leaders of the church are to be an example of self-discipline (1 Peter 5:3). That's why Paul says, "I discipline my body and keep it under control, lest after preaching to others I myself should be disqualified" (1 Corinthians 9:27). It has been said that the piety of a congregation is often proportionate to the piety of the leaders. Self-discipline, therefore, lies at the heart of church discipline. But sanctification is not a solitary exercise. Believers need each other to become complete (Ephesians 4:11–16).

Interpersonal Discipline

Interpersonal discipline takes place when one member of the body offers loving verbal correction to another. It seems today there is great reluctance to begin the work of discipline with another person. Do any of the following excuses sound familiar?

- We believe interpersonal discipline to be hypocritical. After all, you might say, "I have a plank in my own eye. That is, I am guilty of the same sin." If you are indeed stuck in the sin that you like to point out in others, then you *are* a hypocrite! But Jesus has an answer to this: "First take the log out of your own eye, and then you will see clearly to take the speck out of your brother's eye" (Matthew 7:5).

- We avoid interpersonal discipline because we are hyper-resistant to judging. After all, Jesus said, "Don't judge," right? Yes. But he also commands us to "judge with right judgment" (John 7:24). Paul said, "For what have I to do with judging outsiders? Is it not those inside the church whom you are to judge?" (1 Corinthians 5:12). The oft-heard refrain, "Do not judge" is more a commentary on our culture of toleration than it is on the Bible.

- We resist interpersonal discipline because we don't want to offend our friends. Such an objection begs the question, "What is a friend?" God identifies one of the character traits of a Christian as being willing to faithfully wound his friend (Proverbs 27:6). Unwillingness to offer the restoration that comes through conviction and repentance of sin probably indicates that we fear man more than God. It also demonstrates a lack of concern for the well-being of our brother or sister in Christ. *True* friends don't let friends persist in sin.

• We refrain from interpersonal discipline because we don't want to bring scrutiny on our own lives. The "whistleblower" opens himself up to the evaluation of others. "Live and let live" is often a cryptic way of saying, "I'll respect the skeletons in your closet if you respect mine."

The fact is God requires all believers to engage in corrective discipline in the family of God: "If your brother sins against you, go and tell him his fault, between you and him alone" (Matthew 18:15). Don't stew over your brother's sin. Don't gossip about it. Don't continue to hold it against him. Rather than observing these traditional methods of responding to interpersonal conflict, God's answer is "reprove the sinner so he can repent."

But Jesus is not merely holding us accountable to our brothers and sisters when they sin directly against us. Paul generalizes Jesus' instructions: "Brothers, if anyone is caught in any transgression, you who are spiritual should restore him in a spirit of gentleness. Keep watch on yourself, lest you too be tempted" (Galatians 6:1). In response we might say, "Well I'm not spiritual so this verse is not talking to me." If we are indeed not being spiritual but instead "gratify[ing] the desires of the flesh" (Galatians 5:16) then we do have serious matters of our own to attend to and should give urgent attention to them with the help of our spiritual overseers.

The apostle Paul believed that every believer is "full of goodness, filled with all knowledge and able to instruct one another" (Romans 15:14). Paul makes a similar point when writing to the Colossians "Let the word of Christ dwell in you richly, teaching and admonishing one another in all wisdom" (Colossians 3:16). As one writer said, "In both Colossians and Romans, then, Paul pictured

Christians meeting in nouthetic (or admonishing) confrontation as normal everyday activity. He was sure that Christians in Rome were able to do so because they were filled with knowledge and goodness."[3] It was clearly Paul's conviction that much good could be done in the church if believers would take seriously their hortatory responsibilities toward the others in the household of faith.

Church Discipline

If private parties cannot resolve a matter of sin (as is so often the case) it must be brought to the court of the church (Matthew 18:17–20). Christ established this court in Matthew 16 when speaking to Peter and the other pillars of the church: "I will give you the keys of the kingdom of heaven, and whatever you bind on earth shall be bound in heaven, and whatever you loose on earth shall be loosed in heaven" (Matthew 16:18–19; cf. John 20:23). When Paul met with the Ephesian elders he charged them: "Pay careful attention to yourselves and to all the flock, in which the Holy Spirit has made you overseers, to care for the church of God, which he obtained with his own blood" (Acts 20:28). It is the duty of the elders to guide the flock of God through conflict and, if need be, to exclude from the church those who refuse to bend the knee to Christ (1 Corinthians 5:13).

Such exclusion naturally assumes the practice of membership in the local church. Church membership is the "front door" of church discipline while excommunication is the "back door." In order for the shepherds of a congregation to be able to effectively care for the sheep there must be a commitment on the part of the sheep to "promise to submit to the government of the church and, if [they] should become delinquent either in doctrine or in life, to submit to its admonition and discipline"[4] Without such a commitment discipline will simply create a revolving door in the church; those who are disciplined will simply move on to the next church that will accept them.

Before getting to "the back door of discipline" or excommunication, the sanction of discipline should pass through three stages as long as the sinner remain impenitent. First, he should be suspended from the Lord's Supper; a meal meant only for repenting, believing sinners. Second, the sin, and subsequently the sinner, should be brought to the attention of the congregation. Finally, the sinner is formally excommunicated from the fellowship of the church and also, barring subsequent penitence, from the kingdom of God.

Given that the consequences of discipline are so grave, a caution is in order. Church leaders must not rule with an iron fist. Peter exhorts the elders of the church: "Shepherd the flock of God that is among you, exercising oversight, not under compulsion, but willingly, as God would have you; not for shameful gain, but eagerly; not domineering over those in your charge, but being examples to the flock" (1 Peter 5:2–3).

The modern tendency is to write off discipline since, after all, "the church is a place for sinners." This is true. But more accurately, the church is a place for *repentant* sinners. This is the goal of discipline. We need to recover this lost mark of the true church. Many churches today have lost sight of the *spirituality* of *discipline*. Louis Berkhof expressed a very optimistic view of the outcome of discipline when he said, "It is impossible to tell when a process of discipline begins, whether a cure will be effected, or whether the diseased member will finally have to be removed. Probably the church will succeed in bringing the sinner to repentance—and this is, of course, the more desirable end."[5]

We need to recapture the courage of approaching our wavering brother or sister and lovingly explaining to them that what they are doing is sin for which they need to repent. In doing so we need to remember to pray for the person, to love them, and to give them time. As we do so we will more closely resemble the Good

Shepherd and the church will be more perfectly prepared for the wedding supper of the Lamb (Ephesians 5:24–27).

Every congregation of Jesus needs to ask four questions about itself: Who are we as a church? How do we make decisions as a church? How do we relate to other bodies of Christ? What is it we are supposed to be doing? Let's wrestle with these questions. And let's have the humility to recognize our limitations and sins, both personal and corporate. And be renewed by the grace of God that comes through repentance.

Questions

Identify some of the challenges associated with church discipline.

Identify some of the blessings associated with church discipline.

Why is self-discipline a necessary first step in church discipline?

How might 2 Corinthians 5:20 shape our approach to discipline?

Should the early steps of church discipline be swift or slow?

What is excommunication and what are some of its practical implications?

For Further Reading

Jay Adams, *Handbook of Church Discipline* (Grand Rapids: Zondervan, 1974).

URCNA Church Order articles 51–63. https://www.urcna.org/sysfiles/member/custom/file_retrieve.cfm?memberid=1651&custo mid=23868 (Accessed February 17, 2014).

Idzerd Van Dellen and Martin Monsma, *The Church Order Commentary: Being a Brief Explanation of the Church Order of the*

Christian Reformed Church (Grand Rapids: Zondervan, 1941), 291–333.

Conclusion:

The Need for God-Glorifying Church Governance

With all of the responsibilities of life, whether it's being a student, a wife and mother, an owner of a business, or an employee at several jobs to make ends meet, we realize that thinking about church government is one of the least of your worries. But we want you to recall our Lord's saying that the people of Israel were once like "sheep without a shepherd" (Matthew 9:36). What does this vivid image cause your mind to think of? You can imagine a great flock of sheep in a field, some are over here and some are over there. Since there is no shepherd the sheep scatter and wander aimlessly. So what does this mean? Jesus meant to convey that the Israelites had no leaders to provide godly leadership.

Throughout the history of the church the people of God have needed leadership to get them through. When the world was about as depraved as it could be, Noah led a small group to salvation through the Flood. When a famine came upon the land for seven years and it seemed death was to follow, Joseph led Egypt, but also the family of Jacob. When the people spiraled into disobedience, God raised up judges. In the early church, when Arius and his followers were winning the day, a deacon from Alexandria stood up to defend our Lord's deity; and when people said, "Athanasius, the world is against you," he said, "Then Athanasius is against the world!" The church needed leadership then and church needs leadership today. You need to be led; your church needs leaders. Perhaps God is calling you to lead!

Throughout this book we have laid out some of the basics of what a well-ordered and vibrant church of Jesus Christ looks like. We want to conclude where we very well could have begun: the need for such governance of the church. We want to end here because you may be a leader within a church, that needs to be revived in your calling. You may be aspiring to leadership (1 Timothy 3:1). Perhaps you are being considered for future leadership. You may be totally new to a church that takes church government so seriously and want to understand why and how you can better pray for your leaders. We want to encourage and exhort you from Exodus 18:13–27 as we read about the need for God-glorifying church governance in the days of Moses and Israel and how it applies to us.

God-glorifying Governance Is a Need for the People (vv. 13–16)

When the Israelites came out of Egypt there were "six hundred thousand men on foot, besides women and children" (Exodus 12:37). This means that there were roughly 2.5 million Israelites in the wilderness. With that many people the need for leadership was staggering! And with that many sinful people, it wouldn't take long for the pastoral needs to begin to rear their head. Less than three months after the Exodus (cf. 19:1) God's people get a crash-course on the need for God-glorifying governance.

We see how great the needs of the Israelites were, illustrated in two ways in our text. First, their needs are *illustrated in their standing*. The narrator, Moses, says, "and the people stood around

Moses from morning till evening" (Exodus 18:13), and Jethro mentions that, "all the people stand around you from morning till evening" (Exodus 18:14). Second, their needs are *illustrated in their inquiring*. They came and stood for a purpose: to hear what the Lord said about their needs. We hear Moses saying, "the people come to me to inquire of God" (Exodus 18:15).

God-glorifying Governance Is a Need for Current Leaders (vv. 17–18)

We see Moses caught between two needs, in an unenviable, impossible dilemma. This is the dilemma of every church officer: "Do I serve my people's needs or do I serve my own needs?"

Notably, Moses couldn't see his need. By God's grace "Moses' father-in-law said to him, 'What you are doing is not good. You and the people with you will certainly wear yourselves out, for the thing is too heavy for you. You are not able to do it alone'" (Exodus 18:17–18). He needed help. He couldn't do it alone. He wasn't a superman. Sounds like someone you know very well!

At the same time, though, that Moses was to seek assistance so that he might rest and be relieved of the full burden, he was also to provide governance from the Word. Moses himself says, "When they have a dispute, they come to me and I decide between one person and another, and I make them know the statutes of God and his laws" (Exodus 18:16). Then we read what Jethro said about this:

> Now obey my voice; I will give you advice, and God be with you! You shall represent the people before God and bring their cases to God, and you shall warn them about the statutes and the laws, and make them know the way in which they must walk and what they must do. (Exodus 18:19–20)

The leader of Israel needed sufficient respite that he might be a faithful minister of the Word; that he might have sufficient time to read, meditate, and prepare to speak in the name of God.

God-glorifying Governance Is a Need for New Leaders (vv. 21–23)

The minister, Moses, is near burn-out—an experience every minister feels—and the people are also wearing themselves out waiting for their minister alone to speak. So Jethro impresses upon Moses the need for new leaders. He calls upon Moses to "look for able men from all the people" (Exodus 18:21, Cf. 2 Timothy 2:1–2). He goes on to describe what it means to be an "able man" in three ways.

First, new leaders must be men who fear God. To fear God is to have a reverential awe at who he is. It is to know his holiness and thus to know one's own sin. It is to sit as a servant under him as Lord. This is why the Proverbs say the fear of the Lord is the beginning of wisdom (Proverbs 9:10). Without this fear one trusts his own wisdom over God's. But in the church, leaders must trust the Lord and his Word.

Second, new leaders must be men who are trustworthy. This means that since they are going to take some of the responsibility that Moses has, they have to be the kind of men that are able to bear that responsibility and execute their tasks well. They must be worthy of being entrusted "as chiefs of thousands, of hundreds, of fifties, and of tens" (Exodus 18:21). And what a task it is! To govern, lead, and shepherd in the name of Christ is an awesome task.

Third, new leaders must be men who hate a bribe. They cannot seek the pleasure of men over that of God. They cannot fear men more than they fear God. They cannot govern, judge, rule, and lead based on preference and on what they get out of it.

Jethro also impresses upon Moses the blessing of new leaders:

"Every great matter they shall bring to you, but any small matter they shall decide themselves. So it will be easier for you, and they will bear the burden with you," and then he says, "you will be able to endure, and all this people also will go to their place in peace" (Exodus 18:22, 23).

You have spiritual needs, your entire congregation has spiritual needs, your current officers have spiritual needs, and because of this, there is a constant need for new leaders to govern in a God-glorifying way. Will you pray that the Holy Spirit would raise up new leaders and better equip those currently serving? (Numbers 11:29, Acts 6:3). Will you step up and answer God's call to assist your minister? Will you begin preparing yourself for service as an elder, to govern, lead, and shepherd? How are you going to mature your faith and life so that you evidence the fear of God, trustworthiness, and abhorrence of bribes? Will you begin voraciously reading your Bible? Will you study the doctrinal statement(s) of your church? Will you become acquainted with your church's governmental structure? Will you become involved in people's lives so that you know their needs and struggles?

The church has a great need; God has an answer; and God uses sinners like you to bring that answer to fruition that his people will not be like sheep without a shepherd.

Afterword:

Thjs is the sort of book that slips through the cracks. It's not an academic treatise on the doctrine of the church. But it's also not the familiar "how-to" book drawn from the laboratories of business and marketing. Instead, the authors articulate a view of the church's identity, worship, organization and mission that is grounded in the teaching of Scripture.

This in itself is a rather odd approach—at least today. Ironically, many even within self-identified Reformed circles today seem to think that the Bible is the treasure-trove of everything from personal dieting to foreign diplomacy, while suggesting that it has little to say about the practical details of the church's ministry. Just consider the numerous passages that give clear, specific, and normative instruction on the church's ministerial authority, worship, the special offices (pastors, elders, deacons), and the methods for making disciples of "you and your children, and those who are far off" (Acts 2:39). Yet in the history of American evangelicalism especially, these passages have all too often been put on the back-burner. Placed in the category of "Not Gospel Issues," many churches today treat them as if they were insignificant.

One of the things that I like about this book is that the authors just don't believe that at all. In the first place, they believe that

"... teaching them to observe everything that I have commanded" (Matthew 28:20) means *everything*. Christ is the King and whatever he decrees is for our good and the good of the world. Secondly, they believe that the church *is* a "gospel issue." Not everything in the New Testament instructions is at the level of union with Christ and his saving gifts. However, the idea that "getting saved" has nothing to do with "joining a church" is a heresy. And like all heresies, it's not just theoretical but of the utmost practical significance.

Imagine that you are suffering physical pain. You visit your doctor and he tells you that you have cancer. What is your first thought? For most of us, the chief concern is that he or she is qualified to make the diagnosis and to treat the illness. Is our health in this present age more important to us than everlasting life? No Christian would answer affirmatively, of course. But then the question is: To whom do you entrust your everlasting life? Jesus Christ, of course. But then what did Jesus himself say as he was about to ascend to the Father? "Peter, do you love me?" "Yes, you know I do," Peter replied. "Feed my sheep," Jesus said (John 21:17).

The fact that Jesus asked this question three times (matching the three times of Peter's denial of Jesus) underscores the inseparability in our Lord's thoughts between the church and salvation. Only Christ saves us—not the church. And yet, Christ saves us through the ministry of the church. That includes the ministry of pastors who proclaim Christ, in the power of his Spirit; elders who rule, and deacons who serve our physical needs. How richly the Ascended King provides for us, not only in his life, death, and resurrection, but in his ascension, the sending of the Spirit at Pentecost, and the ministry of the apostles. It was these last men who were designated by Christ as his "ambassadors" who, by divine inspiration, laid down the regulations for his ongoing ministry in and through the church. Far from legalistic, these regulations

ensure that we are hearing not merely from men, but from the
Triune God: that is, from the Father, in the Son, by the Spirit.

For all of these reasons—and more, I cannot commend this
book more highly. It fills a very important gap. In fact, it not only
displays familiarity with the great practical works on the church's
ministry from the past; it is in its own right another link in that
chain "from generation to generation."

You may not always agree with the authors. You may think
at times that their interpretations are too strained and that even
the Reformed confessions go too far in thinking that the Bible
addresses such specific issues as how we worship, how the church
is organized, and how it ministers to the baptized and unbaptized
alike. But if you've given them a chance—as I'm assuming you have,
I hope that you (like me) can rejoice in the lavish manner in which
our Lord provides for his church in these last days.

Michael Horton
J. Gresham Machen Professor, Westminster Seminary California

Appendix

Foundational Principles of
Reformed Church Government[1]

1. The church is the possession of Christ, who is the Mediator of the New Covenant.
   Acts 20:28; Ephesians 5:25–27

2. As Mediator of the New Covenant, Christ is the Head of the church.
   Ephesians 1:22–23; 5:23–24; Colossians 1:18

3. Because the church is Christ's possession and He is its Head, the principles governing the church are not a matter of human preference, but of divine revelation.
   Matthew 28:18–20; Colossians 1:18

4. The universal church possesses a spiritual unity in Christ and in the Holy Scriptures.
   Matthew 16:18; Ephesians 2:20; 1 Timothy 3:15; 2 John 9

5. The Lord gave no permanent universal, national or regional offices to His church. The office of elder (presbyter/episkopos) is clearly local in authority and function; thus, Reformed church

government is presbyterial, since the church is governed by elders, not by broader assemblies.

Acts 14:23; 20:17, 28; Titus 1:5

6. In its subjection to its heavenly Head, the local church is governed by Christ from heaven, by means of His Word and Spirit, with the keys of the kingdom which He has given it for that purpose; and it is not subject to rule by sister churches who, with it, are subject to the one Christ.

Matthew 16:19; Acts 20:28–32; Titus 1:5

7. Federative relationships do not belong to the essence or being of the church; rather, they serve the well-being of the church. However, even though churches stand distinctly next to one another, they do not thereby stand disconnectedly alongside one another. Entrance into and departure from a federative relationship is strictly a voluntary matter.

Acts 15:1–35; Romans 15:25–27; Colossians 4:16; Titus 1:5; Revelation 1:11, 20

8. The exercise of a federative relationship is possible only on the basis of unity in faith and in confession.

1 Corinthians 10:14–22; Galatians 1:6–9; Ephesians 4:16–17

9. Member churches meet together in consultation to guard against human imperfections and to benefit from the wisdom of a multitude of counselors in the broader assemblies. The decisions of such assemblies derive their authority from their conformity to the Word of God.

Proverbs 11:14; Acts 15:1–35; 1 Corinthians 13:9–10; 2 Timothy 3:16–17

10. In order to manifest our spiritual unity, local churches should seek the broadest possible contacts with other like-minded

churches for their mutual edification and as an effective witness to the world.

John 17:21–23; Ephesians 4:1–6

11. The church is mandated to exercise its ministry of reconciliation by proclaiming the gospel to the ends of the earth.

Matthew 28:19–20; Acts 1:8; 2 Corinthians 5:18–21

12. Christ cares for His church through the office-bearers whom He chooses.

Acts 6:2–3; 1 Timothy 3:1, 8; 5:17

13. The Scriptures encourage a thorough theological training for the ministers of the Word.

1 Timothy 4:16; 2 Timothy 2:14–16; 3:14; 4:1–5

14. Being the chosen and redeemed people of God, the church, under the supervision of the elders, is called to worship Him according to the Scriptural principles governing worship.

Leviticus 10:1–3; Deuteronomy 12:29–32; Psalm 95:1, 2, 6; Psalm 100:4; John 4:24; 1 Peter 2:9

15. Since the church is the pillar and ground of the truth, it is called through the teaching ministry to build up the people of God in faith.

Deuteronomy 11:19; Ephesians 4:11–16; 1 Timothy 4:6; 2 Timothy 2:2; 3:16–17

16. Christian discipline, arising from God's love for His people, is exercised in the church to correct and strengthen the people of God, maintain the unity and the purity of the church of Christ, and thereby bring honor and glory to God's name.

1 Timothy 5:20; Titus 1:13; Hebrews 12:7–11

17. The exercise of Christian discipline is first of all a personal

duty of every child of God, but when discipline by the church becomes necessary, it must be exercised by the elders of the church, the bearers of the keys of the kingdom.

Matthew 18:15–20; Acts 20:28; 1 Corinthians 5:13; 1 Peter 5:1–3

Bibliography

Wilhelmus à Brakel, *The Christian's Reasonable Service*, trans. Bartel Elshout, ed. Joel R. Beeke, 4 vols. (1992; fourth printing, Grand Rapids: Reformation Heritage Books, 2007).

Jay Adams, *Competent to Counsel* (Grand Rapids: Zondervan, 1970).

——*Preaching with Purpose* (Grand Rapids: Zondervan, 1982).

Herman Bavinck, *Reformed Dogmatics: Holy Spirit, Church, and New Creation*, ed. John Bolt, trans. John Vriend, 4 vols. (Grand Rapids: Baker Academic, 2008).

Joel Beeke, *The Family at Church: Listening to Sermons and Attending Prayer Meetings* (Grand Rapids: Reformation Heritage Books, 2008).

Louis Berkhof, *Systematic Theology* (Grand Rapids: Eerdmans, 1976).

William Boekestein, "Christian Unity (1): Why Should I Care?" *The Outlook* 60:1 (2010): 8.

——, "Christian Unity (2): Exposing Counterfeit Unity" *The Outlook* 60:2 (2010): 7–9.

———, "Christian Unity (3): How Is This Possible?" *The Outlook* 60:3 (2010): 8.

———, "Christian Unity (4): What Must I Do?" *The Outlook* 60:4 (2010): 6–8.

———, "Christian Unity (5): An Encouraging Example." *The Outlook* 60:5 (2010): 5–7.

———, "How to Grow Spiritually." http://www.ligonier.org/blog/how-grow-spiritually/

(Accessed September 1, 2014).

———, *Life Lessons from a Calloused Christian: A Practical Study of Jonah with Questions* (Carbondale, PA: Covenant Reformed Church, 2009).

———, "Profiting from Preaching: Learning to Truly Hear God" *The Outlook* 64:4 (2014): 22–24.

John Calvin, *Institutes of the Christian Religion*, ed. John T. McNeill, trans. Ford Lewis Battles (Philadelphia: The Westminster Press, 1960).

———, *Letters of John Calvin*, trans. Jules Bonnet (Philadelphia: Presbyterian Board of Publication, 1858).

———, *The Necessity of Reforming the Church*, (Edinburgh: The Edinburgh Printing Co., 1843).

Caleb Cangelosi, "The Church is a Missionary Society, and the Spirit of Missions is the Spirit of the Gospel: The Missional Piety of the Southern Presbyterian Tradition." *Puritan Reformed Theological Journal* 5:1 (January 2013): 189–213.

Deborah Rahn Clemens, "Foundations of German Reformed Worship in the Sixteenth Century Palatinate" (Ph.D. diss., Drew University, 1995).

Brandon Cox, "5 Reasons Why the Church Must Engage the World with Social Media." http://christianmediamagazine.com/social-media-2/5-reasons-why-the-church-must-engage-the-world-with-social-media/ (Accessed February 17, 2014).

James J. De Jonge, "Calvin the Liturgist: How 'Calvinist' Is Your Church's Liturgy?" As found at http://www.reformedworship.org/article/september-1988/calvin-liturgist-how-calvinist-your-churchs-liturgy (Accessed February 10, 2014).

Peter De Klerk and Richard De Ridder, eds., *Perspectives on the Christian Reformed Church: Studies in Its History, Theology, and Ecumenicity* (Grand Rapids: Baker Book House, 1983).

Mark Dever, *The Deliberate Church: Building Your Ministry on the Gospel* (Wheaton: Crossway, 2005).

Kevin DeYoung, "A Phrase to Retire." http://thegospelcoalition.org/blogs/kevindeyoung/2011/02/02/a-phrase-to-retire/ (Accessed February 10, 2014).

Ecclesiastical Ordinances in *The Register of the Company of Pastors of Geneva in the Time of Calvin*, ed. and trans. Philip Edgcumbe Hughes (Grand Rapids: Eerdmans, 1966).

W. Robert Godfrey, "A Reformed Dream." http://www.modernreformation.org/default.php?page=articledisplay&var1=ArtRead&var2=123&var3=authorbio&var4=AutRes&var5=70 (Accessed February 10, 2014).

——, *Pleasing God in Our Worship*, Today's Issues (Wheaton: Crossway Books, 1999).

T. David Gordon, "'Equipping' Ministry in Ephesians 4?" *JETS* 37:1 (March 1994): 69–78.

Wm. Heyns, *Handbook for Elders and Deacons: The Nature and the Duties of the Offices According to the Principles of Reformed Church Polity* (Grand Rapids: Wm. B. Eerdmans Publishing Company, 1928).

Charles Hodge, *What is Presbyterianism?* As found at http://www.pcahistory.org/documents/wip.pdf (Accessed February 10, 2014).

Daniel R. Hyde, "According to the Custom of the Ancient Church? Examining the Roots of John Calvin's Liturgy." *Puritan Reformed Journal* 1:2 (June 2009): 189–211 .

——, "From Reformed Dream to Reformed Reality: The Problem and Possibility of Reformed Church Unity." http://theaquilareport.com/from-reformed-dream-to-reformed-reality-the-problem-and-possibility-of-reformed-church-unity/ (Accessed February 10, 2014).

——, *In Living Color: Images of Christ and the Means of Grace* (Grandville: Reformed Fellowship, 2009).

——, "Lost Keys: The Absolution in Reformed Liturgy." *Calvin Theological Journal* 46:1 (April 2011): 140–166.

——, "Rulers and Servants: The Nature of and Qualifications for the Offices of Elder and Deacon," in *Called to Serve: Essays for Elders and Deacons*, ed. Michael G. Brown (Grandville: Reformed Fellowship, 2007), 1–16.

———, *The Nursery of the Holy Spirit: Welcoming Children in Worship* (Eugene, OR: Wipf & Stock, 2014).

———, *Welcome to a Reformed Church: A Guide for Pilgrims* (Orlando: Reformation Trust Publishing, 2010).

Dennis E. Johnson, *The Message of Acts in the History of Redemption* (Phillipsburg: P&R, 1997).

———, "The Peril of Pastors without the Biblical Languages." As found at http://wscal.edu/resource-center/resource/the-peril-of-pastors-without-the-biblical-languages (Accessed July 19, 2014).

Timothy Keller, "Evangelistic Worship." As found at https://theresurgence.com/2011/03/23/evangelistic-worship (Accessed February 15, 2014).

Sean Lucas, *What is Reformed Church Government?* (Phillipsburg, NJ: P&R Publishing, 2009).

Colin Marshall and Tony Payne, *The Trellis and the Vine: The Ministry Mind-shift that Changes Everything* (Kingsford: Matthias Media, 2009).

Will Metzger, *Tell the Truth: The Whole Gospel to the Whole Person by Whole People* (Downer's Grove, IL: Inter-Varsity Press, 1981).

T. H. L. Parker, *Calvin's Preaching* (Edinburgh: T&T Clark, 1992).

Perspectives on the Christian Reformed Church: Studies in Its History, Theology, and Ecumenicity, ed. Peter De Klerk and Richard De Ridder (Grand Rapids: Baker Book House, 1983).

J. I. Packer, *A Quest for Godliness: The Puritan Vision of the Christian Life* (Wheaton: Crossway, 1990).

John Piper and D.A. Carson, *The Pastor as Scholar, and the Scholar as Pastor: Reflections on Life and Ministry* (Wheaton: Crossway, 2011).

Planting, Watering, Growing: Planting Confessionally Reformed Churches in the 21st Century, ed. Daniel R. Hyde and Shane Lems (Grand Rapids: Reformation Heritage Books, 2011).

Randy Pope, *The Prevailing Church* (Chicago: Moody Press, 2002).

Michael Raiter, "The Slow Death of Congregational Singing." As found at http://matthiasmedia.com/briefing/2008/04/the-slow-death-of-congregational-singing-4/ (Accessed February 10, 2014).

Philip Ryken, *City on a Hill: Reclaiming the Biblical Pattern for the Church in the 21st Century* (Chicago: Moody Publishers, 2003).

J. L. Schaver, *The Polity of the Churches, Volume 1: Concerns All the Churches of Christendom* (Chicago: Church Polity Press, 1947).

——, *The Polity of the Churches, Volume 2: Concerns Reformed Churches; More Particularly, One Denomination* (Chicago: Church Polity Press, third edition 1947).

Donald Sinnema, "The Second Sunday Service in the Early Dutch Tradition," *Calvin Theological Journal* 32 (1997): 298–333.

Michael Spotts, "Using Common Media for Church Growth." *Christian Renewal* (May 18, 2011): 25–27.

The Reformed Confessions of the 16th and 17th Centuries in English Translation: Volume 1, 1523–1552, ed. James T. Dennison, Jr. (Grand Rapids: Reformation Heritage Books, 2008).

The Reformed Confessions of the 16th and 17th Centuries in English Translation: Volume 2, 1552–1566, ed. James T. Dennison, Jr. (Grand Rapids: Reformation Heritage Books, 2010).

The Reformed Confessions of the 16th and 17th Centuries in English Translation: Volume 3, 1600–1693, ed. James T. Dennison, Jr. (Grand Rapids: Reformation Heritage Books, 2014).

Paul Tripp, *Age of Opportunity*, (Phillipsburg, NJ: P&R Publishing, 2001).

United Reformed Churches in North America, "Biblical and Confessional View of Missions." As found at https://www.urcna. org/urcna/StudyReports/Biblical%20and%20Confessional%20 View%20of%20Missions.pdf (Accessed February 10, 2014).

———, "Church Order of the United Reformed Churches in North America." As found at https://www.urcna.org/sysfiles/site_ uploads/custom_public/custom2520.pdf (Accessed February 10, 2014).

———, "Office of Deacon in the Churches." As found at https:// www.urcna.org/urcna/StudyReports/Office%20of%20 Deacon%20in%20the%20Churches.pdf.

Timothy Witmer, *The Shepherd Leader* (Phillipsburg: P&R Publishing, 2010).

Endnotes

Introduction

1. Accessed on November 14, 2014, from http://www.joshhunt.com/mail23.htm
2. The Large Catechism, in *The Book of Concord: The Confessions of the Evangelical Lutheran Church*, ed. Robert Kolb and Timothy J. Wengert, trans. Charles Arand, Eric Gritsch, Robert Kolb, William Russell, James Schaaf, Jane Strohl, and Timothy J. Wengert (Minneapolis: Fortress Press, 2000), 380.
3. The principles that help shape this book and which can be found in the appendix, are held in common by the churches of the federation in which we pastor.
4. For a basic description of the classic types of church government (congregational, episcopal, presbyterial), see William Heyns, *Handbook for Elders and Deacons: The Nature and the Duties of the Offices According to the Principles of Reformed Church Polity* (Grand Rapids: William B. Eerdmans Publishing Company, 1928), 32–34; J. L. Schaver, *The Polity of the Churches, Volume 1: Concerns All the Churches of Christendom* (Chicago: Church Polity Press, 1947), 21–63.

Chapter 1

1. Personal references on the following page numbers are attributed to Danny: 19, 41, 53, 65, 68, 79, 91, 101, 113, 125, 137. Those on the following page numbers are attributed to Bill: 46, 72, 84.
2. *The Reformed Confessions of the 16th and 17th Centuries in English Translation:*

Volume 2, 1552–1566, ed. James T. Dennison, Jr. (Grand Rapids: Reformation Heritage Books, 2010), 441.

3. *Reformed Confessions: Volume 2*, 771.

4. From the hymn, "The Church's One Foundation," in *Psalter Hymnal* (Grand Rapids: Board of Publications of the Christian Reformed Church, 1976), #398:1.

5. Philip Ryken, *City on a Hill: Reclaiming the Biblical Pattern for the Church in the 21st Century* (Chicago: Moody Publishers, 2003), 97.

6. Walter Bauer, *A Greek-English Lexicon of the New Testament*, trans. William F. Arndt and F. Wilbur Gingrich, revised F. Wilbur Gingrich and Frederick W. Danker (Chicago: University of Chicago, 1979), 430.

7. *The Reformed Confessions of the 16th and 17th Centuries in English Translation: Volume 1, 1523–1552*, ed. James T. Dennison, Jr. (Grand Rapids: Reformation Heritage Books, 2008), 41.

8. Kevin DeYoung, "A Phrase to Retire." http://thegospelcoalition.org/blogs/kevindeyoung/2011/02/02/a-phrase-to-retire/ (Accessed February 10, 2014).

9. See William Boekestein's "Christian Unity (1): Why Should I Care?" *The Outlook* 60:1 (2010): 8; "Christian Unity (2): Exposing Counterfeit Unity" *The Outlook* 60:2 (2010): 7–9; "Christian Unity (3): How Is This Possible?" *The Outlook* 60:3 (2010): 8; "Christian Unity (4): What Must I Do?" *The Outlook* 60:4 (2010): 6–8; "Christian Unity (5): An Encouraging Example." *The Outlook* 60:5 (2010): 5–7.

10. *Reformed Confessions: Volume 2*, 440.

11. For a classic Protestant explanation of this passage, see John Calvin, *Institutes of the Christian Religion*, ed. John T. McNeill, trans. Ford Lewis Battles (Philadelphia: The Westminster Press, 1960), 4.6.1–7; John Calvin, *Commentary on a Harmony of the Evangelists, Matthew, Mark and Luke: Volume Second*, trans. William Pringle, Calvin's Commentaries, 22 vols. (reprinted, Grand Rapids: Baker Book House, 1996), 16:286–298.

12. Dennis E. Johnson, *The Message of Acts in the History of Redemption* (Phillipsburg: P&R, 1997), 1.

Chapter 2

1. For more on this definition, see Heyns, *Handbook for Elders and Deacons*, 19–20.

2. Louis Berkhof, *Systematic Theology* (Grand Rapids: Eerdmans, 1976), 581. See also Heyns, *Handbook for Elders and Deacons*, 31–32; Schaver, *The Polity of the Churches, Volume 1*, 69–72.

3. *Reformed Confessions: Volume 2*, 443.

4. Berkhof, *Systematic Theology*, 583.

5. *Reformed Confessions: Volume 2*, 442.

6. Mark Dever, *The Deliberate Church: Building Your Ministry on the Gospel* (Wheaton: Crossway, 2005), 131.

7. Chuck Smith, *The Philosophy of Ministry of Calvary Chapel* (Diamond Bar: Logos Media Group, 1992).

8. See Daniel R. Hyde, "Rulers and Servants: The Nature of and Qualifications for the Offices of Elder and Deacon," in *Called to Serve: Essays for Elders and Deacons*, ed. Michael G. Brown (Grandville: Reformed Fellowship, 2007), 1–16.

9. Geoffrey W. Bromily, ed., "oikonomos," in *Theological Dictionary of the New Testament* (Grand Rapids: Eerdmans, 1979), 5:150.

10. Quoted from Rieker in Heyns, *Handbook for Elders and Deacons*, 17–18.

11. John Calvin, *Commentary on a Harmony of the Evangelists, Matthew, Mark, and Luke*, trans. William Pringle, ed. Henry Beveridge, Calvin's Commentaries, 22 vols., (Grand Rapids: Baker, reprinted 1996), Luke 10:16

12. Mark Driscoll, *Confessions of a Reformission Rev.: Hard Lessons from an Emerging Missional Church* (Grand Rapids: Zondervan, 2006), 104–106.

13. Timothy Keller, "Evangelistic Worship." http://download.redeemer.com/pdf/learn/resources/Evangelistic_Worship-Keller.pdf (Accessed November 14, 2014).

Chapter 3

1. *Reformed Confessions: Volume 2*, 443.

2. The Greek term *cheirotoneō* ordinarily is used to say "choose, elect by raising hands." Bauer, *A Greek-English Lexicon of the New Testament*, 881. See also John Calvin, *Commentary upon the Acts of the Apostles*, trans. Christopher Fetherstone, ed. Henry Beveridge, Calvin's Commentaries, 22 vols., (Grand Rapids: Baker, reprinted 1996), 19:27–28.

3. *Psalter Hymnal*, 168.

4. *Psalter Hymnal*, 176.

5. Ryken, *City on a Hill*, 102.

6. Berkhof, *Systematic Theology*, 586.

7. Thomas R. Schreiner, *1, 2 Peter, Jude*, The New American Commentary (Nashville, TN: Broadman & Holman Publishers, 2003), 232.

8. Heyns, *Handbook for Elders and Deacons*, 295

9. On the analogical relationship between the Old and New Testament offices of priest/deacon, king/elder, and prophet/minister, see Daniel R. Hyde, "Rulers and Servants: The Nature of and Qualifications for the Offices of Elder and Deacon," in *Called to Serve: Essays for Elders and Deacons*, ed. Michael G. Brown (Grandville: Reformed Fellowship, 2007), 1–16.

10. *Psalter Hymnal*, 173.

11. Heyns, *Handbook for Elders and Deacons*, 301.

12. Cf. Heyns, *Handbook for Elders and Deacons*, 296.

13. Sean Lucas, *What is Reformed Church Government?* (Phillipsburg, NJ: P&R Publishing, 2009), 22. On the diaconate, see "Office of Deacon in the Churches," at https://www.urcna.org/urcna/StudyReports/Office%20of%20 Deacon%20in%20the%20Churches.pdf

14. Mark Driscoll, *Confessions of a Reformission Rev.: Hard Lessons from an Emerging Missional Church* (Grand Rapids: Zondervan, 2006), 105.

15. Church Order of the United Reformed Churches in North America, arts, 1, 14, 15. https://www.urcna.org/sysfiles/member/custom/file_retrieve.cfm?mem berid=1651&customid=23868 (Accessed February 10, 2014).

16. *Reformed Confessions: Volume 2*, 443.

17. *Psalter Hymnal*, 167–168.

18. *Psalter Hymnal*, 177.

Chapter 4

1. "Now Israel May Say," in *Psalter Hymnal*, 266:1.

2. Herman Bavinck, *Reformed Dogmatics: Holy Spirit, Church, and New Creation*, ed. John Bolt, trans. John Vriend, 4 vols. (Grand Rapids: Baker Academic, 2008), 4:374.

3. "Denomination," in *Concise Oxford English Dictionary* (1911; Oxford: Oxford University Press, Twelfth edition, 2011), 383.

4. For more on this, see Heyns, *Handbook for Elders and Deacons*, 41–48.

5. On this point we are indebted to Dr. Ted Van Raalte for his thoughtful interaction with us.
6. Lucas, *What is Reformed Church Government?*, 19.
7. Schaver, *The Polity of the Churches, Volume 1*, 59–60.
8. See Charles Hodge, *What is Presbyterianism?* http://www.pcahistory.org/documents/wip.pdf (Accessed February 10, 2014).
9. See the "connectional" principle in Lucas, *What is Reformed Church Government?* 26.
10. See Schaver, *The Polity of the Churches, Volume 1*, 83.
11. Schaver, *The Polity of the Churches, Volume 1*, 81.
12. Church Order of the United Reformed Churches in North America, art. 27.
13. J. L. Schaver, *The Polity of the Churches, Volume 2: Concerns Reformed Churches; More Particularly, One Denomination* (Chicago: Church Polity Press, third edition 1947), 107.

Chapter 5

1. Berkhof, *Systematic Theology*, 566.
2. The Church Order of the URCNA says that "Churches are encouraged to pursue ecumenical relations with Reformed congregations outside of the federation which manifest the marks of the true church and demonstrate faithful allegiance to Scripture as summarized in the Three Forms of Unity" (Art. 34).
3. *Letters of John Calvin*, translated Jules Bonnet (Philadelphia: Presbyterian Board of Publication, 1858), 2:348.
4. John Calvin, *Institutes of the Christian Religion* (Grand Rapids: Eerdmans, 1962), 4.2.1.
5. The same can be said of the Second Helvetic Confession (Ch. 17). Louis Berkhof points out that the clear articulation of the marks of the true and false church was a relative innovation of the Reformation era. Due to the splits in the church during the sixteenth century it became necessary to clearly distinguish the marks of the true church from that of the Roman church as well as the various sects that began cropping up. *Systematic Theology*, 576.
6. *Reformed Confessions: Volume 2*, 442.
7. On the issue of the sixteenth-century distinction between "true" and "false"

churches, see Daniel R. Hyde, *With Heart and Mouth: An Exposition of the Belgic Confession* (Grandville, MI: Reformed Fellowship, Inc., 2008), 389–401.

8. *Reformed Confessions: Volume 2*, 849, 850.

9. Part of the membership requirement for the North American Presbyterian and Reformed Council. www.naparc.org (Accessed February 10, 2014).

10. *Reformed Confessions: Volume 2*, 850.

11. "The formation of NAPARC illustrates the 'concentric circle' ecumenical pattern exemplified by John Calvin in the 16th century, that of negotiating with those closest to you in doctrine and in polity before approaching those who are further distant from you." *Perspectives on the Christian Reformed Church: Studies in Its History, Theology, and Ecumenicity*, ed. Peter De Klerk and Richard De Ridder (Grand Rapids: Baker Book House, 1983), 267.

12. Calvin, *Institutes*, 4.2.1.

13. *Reformed Confessions: Volume 2*, 850.

14. Paul would later mention Barnabas as a partner in ministry (1 Corinthians 9:6), and John Mark as a useful and beloved fellow worker (Colossians 4:10, Philemon 24, 2 Timothy 4:11).

Chapter 6

1. *Reformed Confessions: Volume 2*, 777.

2. Ryken, *City on a Hill*, 25.

3. For example, see Dennis E. Johnson, "The Peril of Pastors without the Biblical Languages." As found at http://wscal.edu/resource-center/resource/the-peril-of-pastors-without-the-biblical-languages (Accessed July 19, 2014).

4. See John Piper and D.A. Carson's, *The Pastor as Scholar, and the Scholar as Pastor: Reflections on Life and Ministry* (Wheaton: Crossway, 2011).

5. For the Lord's Day schedule in the Reformation, see the following: in Heidelberg, Deborah Rahn Clemens, "Foundations of German Reformed Worship in the Sixteenth Century Palatinate" (Ph.D. diss., Drew University, 1995), 197–200, 223–258; in Geneva, T. H. L. Parker, *Calvin's Preaching* (Edinburgh: T&T Clark, 1992), 59, cf. *Ecclesiastical Ordinances* in *The Register of the Company of Pastors of Geneva in the Time of Calvin*, ed. and trans. Philip Edgcumbe Hughes (Grand Rapids: Eerdmans, 1966), 40; in the Netherlands, see Donald Sinnema, "The Second Sunday Service in the Early Dutch Tradition," *Calvin Theological Journal* 32 (1997): 298–333.

6. *Reformed Confessions: Volume 2*, 793–794.
7. J. I. Packer, *A Quest for Godliness: The Puritan Vision of the Christian Life* (Wheaton: Crossway, 1990), 221.
8. Cited in Lucas, *What is Church Government?*, 16.
9. For a contrary interpretation of this text, see T. David Gordon, "'Equipping' Ministry in Ephesians 4?" *JETS* 37:1 (March 1994): 69–78) An excellent resource helping church leaders focus on their task as equippers is Colin Marshall and Tony Payne, *The Trellis and the Vine: The Ministry Mind-shift that Changes Everything* (Kingsford: Matthias Media, 2009).
10. A. W. Tozer, *Of God and Men: Cultivating the Divine Human Relationship* (Camp Hill, PA: WingSpread Publishers, 2010), 23.
11. *Psalter Hymnal*, 132.
12. *Psalter Hymnal*, 132–133.
13. See Joel Beeke, *The Family at Church: Listening to Sermons and Attending Prayer Meetings* (Grand Rapids: Reformation Heritage Books, 2008), which offers practical and biblical guidance toward being a learning family in a teaching church.
14. For much practical help in this area see Jay Adams, *Preaching with Purpose* (Grand Rapids: Zondervan, 1982).

Chapter 7

1. Wilhelmus à Brakel, *The Christian's Reasonable Service*, trans. Bartel Elshout, ed. Joel R. Beeke, 4 vols. (1992; fourth printing, Grand Rapids: Reformation Heritage Books, 2007). 1:250.
2. *The Reformed Confessions of the 16th and 17th Centuries in English Translation: Volume 3, 1600–1693*, ed. James T. Dennison, Jr. (Grand Rapids: Reformation Heritage Books, 2014), 124.
3. Calvin, *Commentary* on 1 Peter 2:9.
4. John Calvin, *The Necessity of Reforming the Church*, (Edinburgh: The Edinburgh Printing Co., 1843), 8.
5. Robert Rayburn, "Worship in the Reformed Church." *Presbyterion* 6, no. 1 (Spring 1980): 18.
6. On this, see Daniel R. Hyde, *In Living Color: Images of Christ and the Means of Grace* (Grandville: Reformed Fellowship, 2009).
7. *Institutes*, 1.12.1

8.   *Commentary* on John 4:20.

9.   *Commentary* on John 4:22.

10. W. Robert Godfrey, *Pleasing God in Our Worship*, Today's Issues (Wheaton: Crossway Books, 1999), 27.

11. Godfrey, *Pleasing God in Our Worship*, 28.

12. John Calvin, *Commentary on the Gospel According to John: Volume First*, trans. William Pringle, ed. Henry Beveridge, Calvin's Commentaries, 22 vols. (Grand Rapids: Baker, reprinted 1989), 4:161.

13. John Calvin, *Commentary on A Harmony of the Evangelists, Matthew, Mark, and Luke*, trans. William Pringle, ed. Henry Beveridge, Calvin's Commentaries, 22 vols., (Grand Rapids: Baker, reprinted 1989), Matthew 15:8.

14. "Collect for Purity," *Book of Common Prayer* (1662).

15. R. C. Sproul, *Chosen by God* (Wheaton: Tyndale House Publishers, 1986), 213.

Chapter 8

1.   On children in worship, see Daniel R. Hyde, *The Nursery of the Holy Spirit: Welcoming Children in Worship* (Eugene, OR: Wipf & Stock, 2014).

2.   See James J. De Jonge, "Calvin the Liturgist: How 'Calvinist' Is Your Church's Liturgy?" http://www.reformedworship.org/article/september-1988/calvin-liturgist-how-calvinist-your-churchs-liturgy (Accessed February 10, 2014); Daniel R. Hyde, "According to the Custom of the Ancient Church? Examining the Roots of John Calvin's Liturgy." *Puritan Reformed Journal* 1:2 (June 2009): 189–211.

3.   From the "Directory for Worship" of the Reformed Church in America. https://www.rca.org/page.aspx?pid=1864 (Accessed February 10, 2014).

4.   On the historic Reformed practice of "absolution," see Daniel R Hyde, "Lost Keys: The Absolution in Reformed Liturgy." *Calvin Theological Journal* 46:1 (April 2011): 140–166.

5.   *The Creeds of Christendom*, ed. Philip Schaff, revised David S. Schaff, 3 vols. (1931; repr., Grand Rapids: Baker Books, 1996), 3:832.

6.   See Joyce Borger, "A Delicate Balance." http://www.reformedworship.org/article/june-2011/delicate-balance (Accessed February 10, 2014).

7.   Michael Raiter, "The Slow Death of Congregational Singing." http://

matthiasmedia.com/briefing/2008/04/the-slow-death-of-congregational-singing-4/ (Accessed February 10, 2014).

8. The Collect from the Second Sunday in Advent, *Book of Common Prayer.*

Chapter 9

1. Dave Hunt, *What Love Is This? Calvinism's Misrepresentation of God* (Sisters, OR: Loyal, 2002), 29.

2. This chapter draws heavily from a study committee report entitled "Biblical and Confessional View of Missions" (hereafter, *BCVM*) and is available online: https://www.urcna.org/urcna/StudyReports/Biblical%20and%20 Confessional%20View%20of%20Missions.pdf (Accessed February 10, 2014).

3. *BCVM*, 1

4. *Reformed Confessions: Volume 3,* 131.

5. *BCVM*, 4.

6. *Reformed Confessions: Volume 2,* 789.

7. On this, see Caleb Cangelosi, "The Church is a Missionary Society, and the Spirit of Missions is the Spirit of the Gospel: The Missional Piety of the Southern Presbyterian Tradition." *Puritan Reformed Theological Journal* 5:1 (January 2013): 189–213.

8. See William Boekestein, *Life Lessons from a Calloused Christian: A Practical Study of Jonah with Questions* (Carbondale, PA: Covenant Reformed Church, 2009).

9. Cited in Ryken, *City on a Hill,* 127.

Chapter 10

1. Randy Pope, *The Prevailing Church* (Chicago: Moody Press, 2002), 20, 21.

2. John G. Van Dyke, "Calvinism and the Evangelization of America," in *God-Centered Living: Or Calvinism in Action* (Grant Rapids: Baker Book House, 1951), 72; cf. Berkhof, *Systematic Theology,* 567.

3. C. Peter Wagner, *Strategies for Church Growth* (Ventura, Calif.: Regal, 1987), 168-169.

4. In addition to being a sign of solidarity, "Laying on of hands was a solemn sign of consecration under the law" and still today a "rite agreeing unto order and comeliness ..." John Calvin, *Commentary upon the Acts of the*

Apostles, trans. Christopher Fetherstone, ed. Henry Beveridge, Calvin's Commentaries, 22 vols., (Grand Rapids: Baker, reprinted 1996), 6:6.

5. On the task of church planting, see *Planting, Watering, Growing: Planting Confessionally Reformed Churches in the 21st Century*, ed. Daniel R. Hyde and Shane Lems (Grand Rapids: Reformation Heritage Books, 2011).

6. Listen to William Boekestein's "Developing a Plan for Outreach." http://www.sermonaudio.com/sermoninfo.asp?SID=1024131332313 (Accessed September 1, 2014).

7. On this see Michael Spotts, "Using Common Media for Church Growth." *Christian Renewal* (May 18, 2011): 25–27. David Murray has given a helpful lecture outlining a positive approach to a congregational engagement of social media. http://www.sermonaudio.com/sermoninfo. asp?SID=722131655337 (Accessed on February 17, 2014). See also Brandon Cox's, "5 Reasons Why the Church Must Engage the World with Social Media." http://christianmediamagazine.com/social-media-2/5-reasons-why-the-church-must-engage-the-world-with-social-media/ (Accessed February 17, 2014).

8. See Timothy Witmer's *The Shepherd Leader* (Phillipsburg: P&R Publishing, 2010), where he describes the rich reformed heritage of parish visitation noting, for example that Thomas Chalmers "set out to visit every family in his parish personally. 'It's population was not exactly known, but it was believed to contain somewhere between eleven and twelve thousand souls'" (65).

9. One such resource is Daniel R. Hyde, *Welcome to a Reformed Church: A Guide for Pilgrims* (Orlando: Reformation Trust Publishing, 2010).

10. One of the best is Will Metzger's *Tell the Truth: The Whole Gospel to the Whole Person by Whole People* (Downer's Grove, IL: Inter-Varsity Press, 1981).

11. In 1 Peter, *phobos* is used in reference to God (1:17; 2:17; 3:2*; 3:14) and man (2:18; 3:2*; 3:6) while *prautēs* is used elsewhere only for a wife's gentleness (3:4).

12. Alissa Wilkinson, "The Facebook Market." http://www.worldmag.com/2011/04/the_facebook_market (Accessed February 10, 2014).

Chapter 11

1. *Reformed Confessions: Volume 2*, 776.
2. Berkhof, *Systematic Theology*, 601.

3. Jay Adams, *Competent to Counsel* (Grand Rapids: Zondervan, 1970), 42. One of the words that Paul uses in both of these verses (*noutheteō*) has become the springboard for an entire counseling movement (nouthetic counseling) which seems to have become more useful as it has become more refined.
4. "Public Profession of Faith: Form 1," in *Psalter Hymnal*, 132.
5. Berkhof, *Systematic Theology*, 599.

Appendix

1. These principles are appended to the *Church Order of the United Reformed Churches of North America (URCNA)* and may be found online at http://urcna.org/sysfiles/member/custom/file_retrieve.cfm?memberid=1651&custom id=23868. While these are peculiar to the churches in our own tradition, we believe they apply across the church landscape.

Scripture Index

Confessions Index